DATE DUE

Peace Is the Way Endorsements

"Deepak Chopra envisions a world within our reach where we are the instruments of peace instead of war. *Peace Is the Way* provides practical tools to help us know in our hearts that each one of us matters and is important to the other. In the African tradition of 'Ubuntu,' we say a person is a person through other people. The daily practices suggested in this book offer readers a way to become more fully human and actively engaged as peacemakers in their homes and communities."

DESMOND TUTU
Nobel Peace Laureate 1984, archbishop emeritus of Cape Town, and author of God Has a Dream: A Vision of Hope for Our Time

"I absolutely agree with Dr. Chopra's view that 'if we want to change the world, we have to begin by changing ourselves.'"

HIS HOLINESS THE DALAI LAMA
Nobel Peace Laureate 1989

"The late author-poet Carl Sandburg once wrote, 'Someday there will be a war and no one will come.' How we long for those words to become a reality. Deepak Chopra, who I am honored to call friend, knows the world can change one person at a time. His spiritual compassion shines clearly on every page. Yet Deepak is fully aware of the long, hard struggle necessary to change this cruel world. *Peace Is the Way* is beautifully written and clearly shows nonviolence is the weapon of the strong. Follow his teaching and become a Peace Person. It truly is the only way forward. Thank you, Deepak."

BETTY WILLIAMS
Nobel Peace Laureate 1976, and president and founder of World Centers of Compassion for Children International

"In recent years, the immediate need to counteract aggressive military policies has led many people to neglect their own personal vision of a more peaceful world. In this timely and urgent work, Deepak Chopra argues that there is a way to rise above the engulfing logic of war: that way is peace itself, a spiritual and compassionate approach to humanity that depends on individual transformation. I highly recommend *Peace Is the Way* to all those who want the global peace movement to find its heart again."

OSCAR ARIAS
Nobel Peace Laureate 1987

"Thinking about peace is already a powerful means to contribute to peace. This is the philosophy of Deepak Chopra in his most recent book. I recommend this book to all those who want to create peace."

BOUTROS BOUTROS-GHALI
President of the Egyptian Commission for Human Rights and former secretary-general of the United Nations

"Dr. Chopra's call to take action is coming at a crucial point. One person bearing witness to suffering; one person taking up a cause can indeed make an impact and even save a life. But how revolutionary would it be if everyone believed this? Chopra's call to bring peace to the world through individual action is one that desperately needs to be not only heard, but also believed and acted upon during these troubled times."

DR. WILLIAM F. SCHULZ
Executive Director, Amnesty International USA

"Although I earned my living in the boxing ring, the power of peace has never escaped me, even in my everyday life. In his most recent book, *Peace Is the Way,* Deepak Chopra brings the idea of peace and the power it has over conflict, hatred, and despair into focus. He offers a clear pathway to make this world a better place for all. Deepak often says what you think about and bring into consciousness expands. He invites us all to bring the vision of peace to the forefront of our individual and collective consciousness, where our thoughts will manifest into reality and what a wonderful world this would be."

MUHAMMAD ALI
U.N. Ambassador of Peace

"*Peace Is the Way* in a profound manner shows us that there are creative solutions to the conflict in the world."

DR. MÁRIO SOARES
Former president and prime minister of Portugal

"*Peace Is the Way* goes beyond the customary ways of resolving conflicts, including activism and humanitarianism. It is a bold, creative, and visionary solution to the world's problems."

FEDERICO MAYOR ZARAGOZA
Former director-general of UNESCO and president of UBUNTU (Barcelona)

"I am thankful that Deepak Chopra has enlisted his marvelous gifts as an explorer of the spiritual realm and his demonstrated talents as a skilled mentor in the urgent quest for a way beyond the curse of war. Clearly neither a strictly external nor a purely internal approach will do what needs to be done, and this engagingly written guidebook deftly combines both. It is an invaluable contribution to the most pressing problem of our era."

HARVEY COX
Hollis Professor of Divinity, Harvard, and author of When Jesus Came to Harvard

"I am touched and delighted by Deepak's earnest and lucid message in this timely and essentially useful book. I picked it up and couldn't put it aside. The great thing about it is how simply and clearly he presents the steps to profound personal transformation. He makes it possible—even enchanting—for us to live what we admire. He lifts up once again before our eyes Gandhi's insight that peace is the way, not only the goal, and he fills that so intensely longed-for truth with penetrating points, small and meaningful steps we can take with ease, and reasonable insights. He mobilizes common sense, scientific insight, and spiritual passion to bring within our reach our own personal attainment of the ancient teaching of peace given to us by Moses, Buddha, Laotse, Jesus, Krishna, Muhammad and all the world's great spiritual teachers. Use this book with loving care and you will break free from the drumbeat of desperation all around you! Awaken to your own personal power as a peacemaker!"

ROBERT THURMAN
Jey Tsong Khapa Professor of Indo-Tibetan Buddhist Studies, Columbia University, president of Tibet House US, and author of Inner Revolution *and* Infinite Life.

"The concensus of global wisdom through the ages recognizes that we humans cocreate our living realities through the conduct of our consciousness—we are as we mind. And this global perspective reveals that when we are lodged in the chronic patterns of ego, minding all sorts of individual and cultural pathologies—fragmentation, polarization, violence—cultures of war ensue. And this wisdom presents the prescription for our evolutionary shift to the awakened global consciousness where we live and experience our deep connectivity. Deepak Chopra's latest book, *Peace Is the Way,* speaks to us in a powerful voice that brings this global truth to life for our time. Here he outlines brilliantly how chronic patterns of the violent mentality are etched deeply in the groove of war, and he lays out a pathway to awakening and cultivating more powerful patterns of peace for people of the planet. *Peace Is the Way* is not just another book, but a global manifesto for our time, a script that urgently needs to be heeded and performed by a growing critical mass of earth citizens in our historic passage together from the old destructive ways of ego consciousness to the emerging global consciousness now essential for sustainable and flourishing cultures of peace."

ASHOK GANGADEAN
Professor of philosophy, Haverford College, cofounder-director of the Global Dialogue Institute, coconvenor of the World Commission on Global Consciousness and Spirituality, and author of Meditative Reason, Between Worlds, *and* Awakening of the Global Mind

"Deepak Chopra reminds the politician no less than the philosopher through this book that peace is not something to be found out there but within us, as he addresses the perennial issue of peace with contemporary freshness. He emphasizes that peace is not just the absence of war but the absence of the causes of war itself, and not just in others but also in ourselves. There is no way to peace, peace is the way, otherwise the world goes to pieces."

ARVIND SHARMA
Birks Professor of Comparative Religion, McGill University

"Practical, Empowering, Applicable, Creative, Energizing: *Peace Is the Way* is an inspired prescription to permanently heal the global illness of war. Deepak Chopra transcends religion to lead us on a personal and universal spiritual path of working from the inside out—each and all of us being in peace and actively expressing it in our world. This is the unity of our rising collective consciousness of peace that Deepak so simply and powerfully describes in this world-changing book. I am inspired and grateful."

TOM ZENDER
President of Unity and advisor to the Association for Global New Thought

"*Peace Is the Way* is an excellent book for our troubled times. My grandfather said, 'We must become the change we want to see in the world.' Peace starts with the self and then the whole world joins in."

ARUN GANDHI
Grandson of Mahatma Gandhi and founder and executive director of MK Gandhi Institute for Nonviolence, Memphis, Tennessee

"The essence of our spirituality is very deftly encapsulated in Deepak Chopra's latest sacred scripture, *Peace Is the Way*. This provides the essential ingredients to achieve inner equanimity in order to awaken our soul and the peace inherent in us so that we may manifest it in our external world. A very pragmatic approach far before its time."

BAWA JAIN
Secretary-General of the World Council of Religious Leaders of the Millennium World Peace Summit and chairman of the World Youth Peace Summit

"*Peace Is the Way* shows that the choices that each of us make consciously can shift the structures and power-relations in our globalizing world. This is the only way to create the world that we want."

AHMED KATHRADA
Co-prisoner with Nelson Mandela for twenty-six years and former presidential advisor to Mr. Mandela

"In this time of terrorism, violence, and deprivation, Deepak Chopra's timely book tells us that we must inculcate the habit of peace within ourselves. Then only will it ascend to a collective consciousness, and the peace-maker becomes a pace-maker of global peace."

RAJENDRA M. ABHYANKAR
Ambassador of India to the European Parliament, Belgium, and Luxembourg

"Deepak Chopra elegantly cuts through all the sophisticated nonsense that keeps us locked into thinking that we have no alternative to endless war, that to be 'realistic' is to prepare for the next armed conflict, or that homeland security will be achieved by killing more and more people around the world. Chopra melds the wisdom of his own Hindu tradition with the vision of the Jewish prophets and produces a book that is at once wise and visionary and could, if widely read, contribute to the evolution of consciousness which it predicts."

RABBI MICHAEL LERNER
Rabbi, Beyt Tikkun synagogue, San Francisco, editor of Tikkun *magazine, a bimonthly interfaith critique of politics, culture, and society, and author of* Spirit Matters: Global Healing and the Wisdom of the Soul *and* Healing Israel/Palestine

"In spite of everything we've been conditioned to believe, war isn't necessary! This is Deepak Chopra's urgent and eloquent message. *Peace Is the Way* is a powerful exploration of the most important question facing humankind at this critical moment; how do we bring peace first to ourselves and then to an increasingly violent and dangerous world? Dr. Chopra knows peace inside and out, from the intuitive wisdom of the cell to the projection of fear that prevails on the roiling surface of the world but which doesn't have to. This is a book that can truly change the world one soul at a time."

RABBI ALAN LEW
Director, Makor Or Meditation Center (San Francisco), and author of
This Is Real and You Are Completely Unprepared

"True to the most sacred spiritual teachings, *Peace Is the Way* is a remarkable book on the strength, beauty, and intelligence of peace. Dr. Chopra reminds us of the choices we face every day, inner choices that set us on the path of war or on the path of consciousness and peace. . . . With wit and elegance, wisdom and clarity, he invites all of us to become a bringer of peace. I embrace the realistic and compelling vision of Dr. Chopra who explains the development of peace consciousness as a practical project of personal transformation."

HAL UPLINGER
Television executive and Live Aid producer

"This is a masterpiece revealing the truth behind conflict, war, and terrorism. The way of peace begins within, and here Deepak Chopra wisely guides us and gives us tremendous hope for a better world."

TORKEL FALKENBERG
Director of the Centre for Studies of Complementary Medicine,
Karolinska Institutet, Stockholm, Sweden

"By declaring war on drugs, crime, cancer, and poverty we managed to increase their presence in our lives. A war on terror is having an identical effect. Deepak offers a brilliant alternative in his most compelling book to date."

DR. WAYNE W. DYER
Author of The Power of Intention

"In this brilliant book, Deepak Chopra describes many of the root causes of war and violence, both inner and outer. He prescribes a powerful framework for a way of peace based on ancient wisdom that has never been so relevant. *Peace Is the Way* is a call to action that can make a real difference in our survival, one person at a time. This may be the most meaningful book of the year."

DEAN ORNISH, M.D.
Founder and president of the Preventive Medicine Research Institute, Clinical Professor of Medicine, University of California, San Francisco, and author of Dr. Dean Ornish's Program for Reversing Heart Disease *and* Love and Survival

"Deepak Chopra believes in peace over war, and hope over despair, for ethical, moral, as well as practical reasons. Deepak advocates and accomplishes without reservation, hesitation, or equivocation a world for all of us whereby peace isn't just *the* way—it's the *only* way."

DAN GLICKMAN
President and CEO of the Motion Picture Association of America

"*Peace Is the Way* clearly shows us how to bring peace to the world by generating it from within ourselves. I believe this is not only the most spiritual and practical approach but also the most artful way of living—as we are all creative beings in a creative universe."

PETER MAX
Artist

"I realize through the pain of losing my wife and daughter on September 11, that this paradigm espoused by Deepak is a moral imperative for all governments of the world to read and should be the cornerstone of our foreign policy if our species is to survive."

DAVID MCCOURT
Father of Juliana, husband of Ruth, and friend to Paige Farley-Hackel, passengers on hijacked flights American Airlines 11 and United Airlines 175, which struck the World Trade Center on September 11, 2001

"The pain of war is ugly and unbearable. How can the death of thousands of innocent victims and soldiers be a vehicle to peace? *Peace Is the Way* shows the way to people's hearts and souls."

LYNN BRADACH
Mother of Travis Bradach-Nall, U.S. Marine killed by a "friendly cluster bomb" in Iraq

"Once again, Dr. Chopra has given us a prescription to bring out our highest selves. The choice is ours whether we choose to follow his recommended practice for making peace real in our personal lives. This may be one of the ultimate choices each of us makes for the future of our world. Out of the simplicity of 'Seven Practices for Peace' will come profound shifts toward world peace. My son Josh once told me, 'Mom, go to your heart and make all your decisions from there and all will be well.' Deepak's *Peace Is the Way* gives me new perspective on these words of wisdom. The way to peace is through the heart."

NANCY H. ROTHSTEIN
Evolving peacemaker, author, and mother of Joshua, who was struck and killed by an automobile at age 15½

PEACE IS

<u>Bringing War and</u>

DEEPAK
CHOPRA

THE WAY

Violence to an End

Harmony Books

NEW YORK

Endpaper photograph courtesy of Image State/Alamy

Copyright © 2005 by Deepak Chopra

Published by Harmony Books, an imprint of the Crown Publishing Group,
a division of Random House, Inc.
www.randomhouse.com

HARMONY BOOKS is a registered trademark and the Harmony Books colophon
is a trademark of Random House, Inc.

Printed in the United States of America

Design by Lynne Amft

Library of Congress Cataloging-in-Publication Data is available upon request

ISBN 0-307-23607-2

10 9 8 7 6 5 4 3 2 1

First Edition

To all the peacemakers in the world
who by becoming firmly established in nonviolence will cause
all beings around them to cease to feel hostility.

Acknowledgments

PETER GUZZARDI, my skillful editor: you are both my critic and one of my best friends;

Shaye, Julie, Julia, Tina, Tara, Brian, Jenny, Sarah, and the rest of my family at Harmony: you have been loving, gracious, and tolerant since the beginning of my career;

Roberto Savio and Arsenio Rodriguez, you have made the Alliance for the New Humanity something to be proud of;

Rita, Mallika, Gotham, Sumant, Candice, and my darling Tara and Leela: you make everything worthwhile and sacred;

Carolyn Rangel, Felicia Rangel, and Janice Crawford in my office: your dedication and hard work make everything possible;

And finally, thanks to my family at the Chopra Center, who translate my words into a practice that makes a difference in people's lives.

Contents

Contents

THE POLITICS OF THE SOUL

(STILL) MAD AS HELL

WHY DOES GOD WANT WAR?

THE METAPHYSICS OF TERROR

THE BODY AT PEACE

OUR BEST HOPE

"There is no way to peace. Peace is the way."

MAHATMA GANDHI

WAR ENDS TODAY

TODAY IS A good day for war to come to an end.

The symbolic number of 1,000 U.S. casualties was passed today in Iraq—I am writing this on September 9, 2004—most of the deaths occurring after victory was declared over a year ago. What is the world like on the day you read this? I cannot predict, but I know, even if this particular war is over, you will be confronted with terrorism, suicide bombings, insurrections and civil war somewhere on the planet, and nuclear threats from U.S.-labeled "rogue" nations like North Korea and Iran. Violence will still be raging out of control, no matter what day you read these words.

AT THE OUTSET of 2003 it was estimated that thirty military conflicts were being fought around the world. It's a good day for all these wars to come to an end. But will they? And if they do, what will replace them?

To end war, you have to think of ending not just one conflict, and not just thirty. What we have to end is the idea of war, which has turned into the habit of war, and then into the numbing constancy of war. The last time the U.S. wasn't on a war footing was December 6, 1941, the day before Pearl Harbor inflamed the U.S. into declaring war against Japan. Since then, America has accepted the need for a huge standing army, the growth of arms manufacturers and merchants into a massive part of the economy, thousands of troops stationed around the world, intensive research into new technologies of death, and a political climate in which it is suicide to come out against war. This whole situation, which reaches into every home, keeps us on a war footing even when there is no declared war to grab the headlines.

Like any habit, war has worn a groove in our minds, so that when we become very afraid or very angry, the response of war comes naturally. It has an easy track to follow. Even as the body count rises in the Sunni Triangle and the photographs of torture from Abu Ghraib prison stun one's conscience, the groove is still there, deep and familiar. War has almost become a secret pleasure. It brings excitement and revs up the routine pace of life. In Mira Nair's film adaptation of *Vanity Fair*, a woman comments smugly at a party, "War is good for men. It's like turning over the soil." We reach for war the way a chain-smoker reaches for a cigarette, muttering all the while that we have to quit. In the past four decades America's war habit has led us into Iraq, Afghanistan, Kuwait, Somalia, Lebanon, Panama, Grenada, Vietnam, and Cambodia, not to mention more covert military operations into places like Laos, Nicaragua, and Colombia.

This book is about erasing that groove and substituting a new way to respond when we are very afraid or very angry, or even when we aren't. The way of peace has to become a new habit. To do that, it must offer a substitute for every single thing that war now provides. You may feel immune to the appeal of war, but everyone has benefited from war's gifts in some measure.

War provides an outlet for national vengeance.

It satisfies the demands of fear.

It brings power to the victor.

It provides security to the homeland.

It opens an avenue for getting what you want by force.

By contrast, living in peace one breathes easily. There is space to allow for connections with other people. Arguments proceed with mutual respect for either side. Mahatma Gandhi, Nelson Mandela, and Mother Teresa lived different aspects of peace. We learned from each that the way of peace can end suffering and oppression, not by warring against an enemy but by bearing witness to wrongs, and by allowing sympathy and common humanity to do their patient work. War smothers all of that.

War's gifts may prove bitter and empty in the end, but that hasn't eroded the groove of war in our minds. Today, after a century in which more than 100 million people died from war, we survivors still turn to war because we think it does some good. The satisfaction of waging war cannot be replaced by philosophy or religion. The Buddha and the Prince of Peace could not have spoken out more strongly against violence, yet their beliefs have been distorted into a cause for bloodshed at the hands of their followers.

Our age is steeped in mechanized warfare that is totally terrifying in human terms. Somewhere in this country teams of scientists are working on a bomb that will vaporize human beings on contact without destroying the buildings they inhabit. Somewhere in this country other scientists are figuring out how to disrupt an enemy's water, electricity, communications, and transportation using signals delivered by the Internet. Soon we may be able to cripple other nations without even having to set foot in them.

We are almost there now, thanks to high-altitude pinpoint

bombing and long-range "smart bombs" that can guide themselves to their targets while our soldiers remain safely out of harm's reach. This technology makes some people, even in the military, very queasy, for it means that our army can kill at leisure without loss of life on our side. The last vestige of honor on the battlefield was respect for the enemy, but no more. The satisfaction of managing death so efficiently has to be added to the list of war's gifts.

Can the way of peace really substitute for all that? Can it succeed where centuries of wisdom and morality have failed?

It can, because the way of peace isn't based on religion or morality. It doesn't ask us to become saints overnight, or to renounce our feelings of anger or our thirst for revenge. What it asks for is something new: conscious evolution.

The time has come for us to stop being passive, and to take control of our own destiny, one person at a time. What keeps war alive? Backwardness of response, a reliance on reactions that human beings have followed since the beginning of history. Violence is not the essence of human nature. It is prevalent, yes, and it is innate. But so is the opposite of violence: love. The way of peace is love in action. Although humankind, explicitly or implicitly, seems to believe that violence is more powerful than love, this is the same as saying that death is more powerful than life.

That simply isn't so. Humanity has evolved to transcend many things that once seemed innate. We have learned to use reason triumphantly. We have overcome superstition and disease. We have exposed the darkness of the psyche to light. We have delved deep into the workings of nature. All these successes point the way to the next step, which is the realization that human beings have outgrown war.

Today isn't the day that I or anyone else can say that human beings are finally and forever beyond war. The only recent news item that gives hope is a small one, a piece of reported data which says that the last twelve months, despite the headlines from Iraq, brought the fewest deaths in war since 1945, the end of World War II. The total body count from all conflicts over the last year was 20,000 worldwide. So the trend may be starting already. You and I, in our anguish to end war, may be catching tremors from the future.

Today is the day to act on them. Just as Newton's formulation of gravity meant that human beings were finally and forever on the road of a new science, a road that has led to a completely transformed world, you and I can create a new turning point. I would argue that for the majority of people in America—and many other parts of the world—the tide of the future has turned already. People are ready to follow the way of peace, if only they can learn what it is.

The way of peace is based on the same thing that ushered in the age of science: a leap in consciousness. When they witnessed demonstrations of steam engines, electric lights, and vaccines, people adapted to them at the level of their own awareness. The idea of being human could no longer be consistent with reading by candlelight, traveling by horse, suffering through high rates of death in childbirth, short life spans, and the ravages of disease. A leap in collective consciousness took place.

The way of peace, I believe, can change the future in the same way. If you and I demonstrate that peace is more satisfying than war, the collective consciousness will shift. Today you and I woke up and found it easy not to kill anyone. Our society, however, can't say the same. It's time for society to take a direction that conforms to what the individual wants. There can be no excuse for living our comfortable lives embedded in a culture of mechanized death and violence. You and I are not innocent bystanders to war. We depend upon it politically, economically, and socially. I will show in detail why this is true, and how we can shift our allegiance to a way of life that is not entangled in war or death. The more people who join us, the faster war will come to an end. Instead of wishing that others would stop killing, you can become a force for peace, and in so doing make the ultimate contribution.

If you shift your allegiance to peace, war ends for you today. This happens one person at a time, but it works. A million tiny earthquakes move more ground than a single cataclysmic quake. There is no better or easier way to live than by catching the wave of evolution. How hard is it to look up and say, Today is a good day for war to end. If your consciousness follows these words and remains true to them, war will never return to your life again.

THE WAY OF PEACE

MAHATMA GANDHI EXPRESSED a profound truth when he said, "There is no way to peace. Peace is the way." What he meant is that peace isn't achieved by working with violence or working through it. Peace has its own power, its own scheme for organizing events. We are looking for substitutes that can satisfy needs that are now being satisfied by war. The old satisfactions aren't trivial, for adventure, power, and expansion are primary values in life.

If there is no viable way for the average person to participate in adventure, power, and expansion, then even the illusory way of war, with its terrible toll in human life, is preferable to nothing. As we'll see, if you go deep enough into the way of peace, you find power. You achieve the freedom and excitement that adventure is supposed to bring. You expand in consciousness without having to invade another country and seize its riches. War is above all a material thing. It involves brute force, bodies fighting against bodies, the destruction of cities that get rebuilt, the squandering of weapons so that more deadly ones can be devised.

If people could achieve satisfaction without destruction, I believe they would. Millions of us want to live without destruction already. Now we are looking for a way to make our will and desire more powerful than war. Fortunately, that isn't complicated. According to the ancient Vedic texts, you will know you are living the way of peace when three things are present:

Seva: Your actions harm no one and benefit everyone.
Simran: You remember your true nature and your purpose for being here.
Satsang: You belong in the community of peace and wisdom.

These three S-words come from Sanskrit. They describe the ideal life of any spiritual person. But just as crucial, they unlock a power that materialism can't defeat, as a rock can't defeat the rain even though one is hard and the other soft, as a tree can't defeat the wind, even though one is solid and the other invisible. Power can sound abstract, but satisfaction isn't. With each S-word comes a satisfaction that war will never be able to match.

Seva brings the joy of knowing that your daily actions support life as a whole. You become part of the planet's evolution, not its wholesale destruction. You live in peace with your conscience because you have fulfilled your duty to be a steward of every aspect of Nature, down to the most sacred level.

Simran brings the satisfaction of expanded possibilities. You are not limited to being one individual lost in a sea of humanity. You find your authentic self and your authentic truth. A unique path to mastery is opened for you and you alone.

Satsang brings the satisfaction of having no enemies. You are at home in the world. The rest of the human family is part of you. Older and younger generations are no longer separated by a gap but work together toward the vision of a world without poverty, ignorance, and violence.

The prime reason that peace is the trend of the future is that all three of these things are already strong trends themselves. By some estimates between a third and a half of Americans accept some form of New Age values, a broad enough spectrum so that it's no longer useful to even use that label. What is useful is to see that you matter and are not alone. In 1987 a housewife walking in the rain to get bread in the shadow of the Berlin Wall might have had no idea that her suppressed will to be free was more potent than the wall. What is one person's will compared to bricks, machine gun towers, and barbed wire? But will is an aspect of consciousness, and the trend of time must obey consciousness when it decides to change. Your suppressed will, I believe, is already shaping the future, even though you are only engaged in everyday things like walking through the rain to buy some bread. Here is just a sample:

TRENDS OF A NEW HUMANITY

The vision that already unites us

Do you believe the world needs to unite around global warming?

Do you want to see a major effort to end AIDS worldwide?

Do you want to see the oceans free of pollution?

Do you think America should lead the Third World to achieve sustainable economies?

Do you defend freedom of religion and an end to religious fanaticism in all its forms?

Do you want full equality of rights for immigrants?

Do you want to see an end to all nuclear stockpiles?

Do you want to see America become less militarized?

Do you want to see an alternative to fossil fuels developed as
quickly as possible?

Do you believe in the equality of women in every society?

Decades of striving may lie ahead before these goals become reality, but as accepted beliefs they are already alive and vital. Millions of people who have no identification with the New Age,
who have never marched in a demonstration for equal rights or
against corporate pollution, who regard themselves as centrists in
social policy, are in fact part of a majority waiting to recognize
itself. The way of peace includes all these objectives, since each
one falls under the category of service for the common good
(Seva), a shift in self-image to a higher level (Simran), or erasing
differences to bring about a new human community (Satsang).

The surprise, really, is that the way of peace hasn't gathered
more momentum. I can see some of the obstacles that have
refused to move. The massive buildup of arms over the last fifty
years appears to be unstoppable. The authorities who control
those arms feel no compunction about using intimidation and
fear to advance their agendas. The overwhelming dominance of
greedy corporations driven by no values except competition and
profits creates its own intimidation. In various ways these forces
prevent spiritual people from thinking they have any power. We
can be honest about that with each other. People feel timid about
stepping out from the crowd and being labeled as different, and
there's a dread of being isolated when you cannot find others
who believe as you do.

Set your timidity aside for a moment and realize something
that's surprising but true. Materialistic obstacles are beside the
point. They exist at a level that may be convincing in appearance

but has little effect on our hearts and our deepest desires. *You are potentially more powerful than any weapon.* I realize that this is a great leap for people to take. Think back on the vast May Day parades rumbling through Red Square in the Soviet era, flaunting an enormous display of missiles and tanks. The facade looked invulnerable. Now we know better than to believe the displays of might. Behind those steel masks the structure of Communism was crumbling, which is why, in this country, we see similar overblown efforts to convince people that they must respect and obey the old pro-war system. Armaments are real, but they cannot stop the birthing of new beliefs.

The secret strength of peace is precisely that it isn't materialistic. If you commit yourself to having even a fraction of extra confidence in the future, you will stop feeling weak and alone. Be assured, consciousness is on the move. Try and absorb that fact and what it implies. Spiritual communities have sprung up around the world to consciously guide the future. In this country every sizable town has alternative churches whose congregations follow a vision that includes Seva, Simran, and Satsang in various forms. But there is no need to exclude mainstream society, which already accepts many aspects of these spiritual values. Let me list some key words.

Seva—selfless action: charity, volunteerism, school outreach programs, mentoring, healing, animal rights, conscientious objectors, evangelism.

All of these movements express a desire to offer service through altruistic actions. They are not motivated by money or a need to be self-important. There is an underlying belief that the ones performing the service are doing as much good for themselves as for those they help. Seva represents the impulse to break out of the traps of ego, selfishness, and money.

Simran—higher vision of humanity: environmentalism,

the peace movement, human rights, psychotherapy, alternative medicine, the human potential movement, Eastern and New Age religions.

All of these movements are linked by a higher vision of what it means to be human. They oppose a technological society in which the individual is diminished and dehumanized. Official doctrines are being challenged. Simran expresses the impulse to live in spiritual dignity, purity, and upliftment.

Satsang—communities of peace and wisdom: churches, prayer groups, peace vigils, convents, monasteries, meditation retreats, communes and cooperatives, utopian communities.

All of these groups are united by a desire to find a new way to live together. They are a reaction to the anonymity of cities and the breakdown of real human connections. Churches, of course, have existed for thousands of years, but there is never a shortage of new groups motivated by new beliefs. Satsang expresses the impulse to share one's spiritual journey with others, to give physical form to the human family.

It may seem strange to put evangelism on the same list as conscientious objectors and the human rights movement, but a fervent Baptist urging others to find Christ is expressing the same spiritual longing as a utopian New Age community under the shadow of Mount Shasta. *Reborn* is a valid word for what millions of people feel they want, often with desperate urgency, even if one rebirth is wildly different from another. America has a deep, inclusive tradition, and there is not a single era going back to the Pilgrims when utopian communities didn't exist here. Many people have lost sight of this, believing that middle-class comfort is the reason for America to exist. But to think that, you'd have to turn your back on centuries of spiritual vision. The way of peace isn't a revolution. It's a consolidation of everything that's already here.

The status quo is mounting a massive effort to deny and repudiate this new growth; it wouldn't be the status quo if it didn't. The most damaging repudiation by far is war. If war can be sustained, the dominance of the old order is assured. By old order I don't mean a social order but literally the way in which we order our world. At the present moment the world is ordered along values of power and force, economic competition, ruthless progress at the cost of traditional society, and the onward march of technology. Figure 1 expresses the old order as a tangled web of trends and values.

This chart displays reality as a tangled hierarchy, a phrase I've borrowed from physics, which sees the whole cosmos as a tangle of matter and energy. It's overwhelming to see how much

Figure 1.

damage has been done to a higher vision of humanity. The tangled hierarchy is our creation. We have all contributed to building some part of it through fear, greed, and unsustainable growth.

Whenever this chart is thrown up as a slide on a screen, every audience reacts with gasps and groans. These trends intertwining with each other like snakes are tightly interrelated. You can take any two topics, no matter how far apart they are on the chart, and link them together. I'd like you to pause a moment to do that, because this tangle of factors is the real enemy, not any single item. Choose any set of pairs picked at random and think of a link between them. For example:

Fossil fuels + Religious conflict: These are linked by war in Iraq.

Extinction of species + Pollution-related diseases: These are linked by the mushroom growth of industrialized cities around the world.

Greed + Water shortage: These are linked by hydroelectric dams that stifle rivers in order to service big cities.

Religious fundamentalism + Gun industry: These are linked by a belief that God wants true followers to kill infidels or to defend themselves in the coming Apocalypse.

I've picked four pairs, but potentially this chart yields several hundred. We live in a totally interdependent world. Trying to attack one problem at a time is futile. In practical terms, this chart is the living proof of Gandhi's declaration that there is no way to peace. There can't be when reality is this tangled and every problem has an incestuous relationship with every other.

I asked you to think of one link for the pair you picked, but there are actually innumerable links. Greed and water shortage is about rivers, dams, treaties, competition between states, corporate pollution, and growing urban areas that outstrip the available water supply. You could archive a hundred news stories a day pertaining to this pair just in the U.S. alone. For the pair that links fossil fuels and religious conflict you could archive a thousand stories a day.

You have seen what is meant by the old order. It's an entire world. Now consider a second chart (Figure 2) that displays a different world.

This is also a tangled hierarchy, only instead of being based on fear and greed, it expresses peace consciousness. As with the first chart, everything here is interrelated. For each item there is a movement that already exists, and across the board there are shared human values. Whenever I display this chart, audiences react with surprise and renewed hope. Although the world constructed from fear and greed is extremely intimidating, it isn't

Figure 2.

the whole world. Human beings are complex, and we are each contributing to a second world that is just as real as and far more sustainable than the first.

I'd like you to choose a few pairs from this chart and link them. For example:

Shared suffering + Healthy community: These two are linked by the 9/11 tragedy and the bonds it formed among victims' families.

Recycling + Better quality of life: These two are linked by the reduction of polluted water in towns that do not indiscriminately bury waste in landfills.

Sense of the sacred + Holistic education: These two are linked by private school systems that teach children from a spiritual basis.

One can make hundreds of pairs from this chart, as with the first, and countless connections. This implies that the new world is already complete, which is true. There is no lack of outlets for peace consciousness, rooted as they are in love and sharing. Those values have been alive for centuries. The major difference between the two worlds I've pictured is consciousness. Fear and greed emanate from a lower level of consciousness, a level we all participate in. Love and sharing emanate from a higher level of consciousness, also one in which we all participate.

The critical question, then, is which level you want to give your allegiance to.

The notion that the world will change if enough people raise their consciousness is absolutely true. The world of fear and greed didn't come about by accident. You and I experience such a world entirely built by consciousness. If we want a new world, we are at a huge advantage in knowing what it means to create a shift in consciousness. Let's go deeper into this notion, because the phrase *shift in consciousness* sounds thin and tired to many people. It echoes an idealism that never seems to get anywhere. It sounds like a philosophy that is content to sit on the sidelines, being in this world but not of it. That is far from the truth, however.

HOW TO BIRTH A WORLD

Seven building blocks of reality

Thought and belief
Emotions
Intentions
Relationships
Turning points and breakthroughs
Environment
Vision

These factors must be alive and active in order for any world to be born, not just the new one we want to create for peace. Whenever consciousness is ready for a shift, you will see ferment and turmoil in all these areas. The established order will be challenged, and working from the silent and invisible level of consciousness, a new order will begin to emerge. It feels like a mystical process, because no one controls the switch and yet everyone does. A common desire wakes up without people knowing that they are invisibly linked.

This truth came home to me when my son Gotham was a teenager. He is the offspring of immigrants, a devotee since childhood of Lord Krishna (whom he first knew from devouring Indian comic books featuring the exploits of gods and goddesses), and a boy invisibly linked to a deep tradition. When our family rose to do morning *puja* with rice and incense, our little household ceremony was one stitch in the millions that preceded it. But at the same time, to the immense relief of his mother and me, Gotham worshiped basketball and would have died for his beloved Celtics—new links were invisibly tying him to this country. Then one day he and I were chatting, and I had the sense that my child had no comprehension of war. I remember being struck with the strangeness of it. We were discussing Vietnam, which ended before he was born, and his face showed me that he had drawn a bank. *Why did they fight? What was all the anger and turmoil over?* So I asked him if he could think of a good reason to go to war, and all Gotham could do was shrug. In some region of consciousness an old link had broken, and everything that war offered to older generations—adventure, romance, a testing ground for machismo, a stage for the drama of good versus evil—no longer mattered. I hasten to add that my son wasn't apathetic; he grew up to become a journalist who travels to many of the hottest war zones reporting back with great curiosity and compassion on this obsession with war that he, to this day, cannot understand because the connection is broken.

If you look around, you'll see the same phenomenon. The birthing process of the future doesn't have to be mystical. The needed skills to break with the past have always existed in us. But the new world that is now emerging, one based on peace, will be unique. Other worlds were born because of shared religions (the Christian Middle Ages, for example) or shared technology (Western industrialism, for example), but none was completely global. The key words that will define the new hierarchy are:

Conscious evolution
Self-determination
Nonmilitary

Nonsectarian
Global sharing
Sustainable economies
Healed environments

These separate trends are going to link and fuse as they coalesce. The same thing has already happened to you biologically, only you don't remember it. An embryo starts life in the mother's womb as a loose blob of cells, and with time one witnesses increased complexity. Cells coalesce into organs, these organs communicate and sense that they are part of the whole. Intelligence takes over to keep the embryo intact; by the final months of pregnancy new neural connections form at the rate of millions per minute. Eventually the fetus is so complex that it has no choice but to be born—a goal that nature always had in mind but that was impossible until there was sufficient order and power inside the embryo for it to become independent. Social orders follow the same pattern before birth. People say, "I already believe in all these things you've listed. Why aren't they real yet?" I sense the discouraging answers they are giving to themselves inside: *No one can beat the system, the problems are too huge, males are innately violent, human nature has always been self-destructive, there's too much ignorance in the world.*

These obstacles are phantoms. They were just as present before the rise of Christianity, yet a Christian world was born from thirteen people. The barriers of ignorance and superstition existed in every society before the arrival of science and technology, but Newton's apple gave rise to the world we now inhabit. The real answer to why we don't see a new world yet is that it isn't ready to be born. It won't be ready until the building blocks become stronger.

REALIZING OUR POWER

Using awareness to shape time

Thought and belief. If you believe in something strongly enough, you will begin to see it. Reality is built from the most subtle level: a fleeting intuition or wish, a desire that won't go away. Thinking about peace is a powerful means to make it happen if that thought comes from a deep level. Jesus and Buddha were many things, but most importantly they were thinkers who believed that their mental processes could alter reality.

You possess the very same tools, only you haven't turned them to changing reality.

Emotions. Currently most people use their emotions for discharge. Pent-up anger and anxiety need an outlet. But freed emotion is far more powerful. Feeling carries truth. The mind can rationalize living in a mechanized culture rife with the technology of death, but our emotions say otherwise. They want to flow in freedom, without anxiety and the constant need to be vigilant for enemies. This level of consciousness recognizes any chance to find increasing happiness and fulfillment. In that regard emotions are an extremely reliable guide. To feel the anguish of war and compassion for its victims is a force that wants to create change.

Intentions. By themselves, thoughts and emotions are loose and free-floating. To give them a purpose, the element of intention must be added. Intention is more than a direction, a way you want to go. If it comes from a deep level, an intention clears the way for its own fulfillment. As if from nowhere, events begin to organize themselves to turn thoughts into reality. Intentions are most powerful when they are positive and creative. Merely wanting bad things to stop isn't enough. You must intend something new to replace the old. A peace movement that is only anti-war has never succeeded. We must envision an entirely new order based on peace, and then unseen forces will start to gestate that reality.

Relationships. The previous elements all came from the inside. Consciousness isn't just an internal phenomenon, however. It needs to flow outward, and this happens through relationships. You can't bring about a peaceful world except by relating peacefully. Relationships are the crucible of reality. They test by fire whether someone is really free of violence, whether peaceful solutions can be found to tough problems, whether an ideal is actually viable in the rough and tumble of the marketplace. A world at peace comes about once we relate to each other as peaceful beings, one individual at a time.

Turning points and breakthroughs. As consciousness does its work, the seams of the old order begin to weaken. Here and there they break apart. At those moments, a person experiences a personal breakthrough. This is proof that consciousness has been paying attention. Old patterns rupture and you begin to see light in place of darkness. Breakthroughs happen because the earlier building blocks have done their job. In the first chapter I cited a small passing news story about 2003 having fewer war deaths than any year since the end of Word War II. I'd consider that a breakthrough, not a random event. It could be as significant as the fall of the Berlin Wall, which I would call a turning point. A breakthrough gives a glimpse of light; a turning point actually alters the shape of time. The peace movement needs to pay attention to breakthroughs and share them around the world.

Environment. Few people doubt that the environment is sick, wounded by the reckless disregard of human beings. The physical world is mirroring our own wounds; its sickness began inside us. When there are enough people who have healed themselves, the environment will also mirror that. I am not speaking of policy changes and adopting the Kyoto accord. Nature is a living expression of consciousness. It adapts to our evolution as we adapt to it. That relationship, as with everything in the tangled hierarchy, is reciprocal and interdependent. It's disturbing that so much of New Age thought is centered on catastrophic earth changes, such as earthquakes and the depleted ozone layer. This kind of prophetic negativity cannot attain a good end. It encourages the prophecy to come true when what we want to do is exactly the opposite. The principle to keep in mind is that consciousness *wants* to evolve. Therefore it is much easier to encourage healing than to align yourself with disease. Love and respect for the environment would create a reversal of the spiraling deterioration in the physical world. We need to trust that this is true, because in a very real sense the environment is sustained by human awareness. If you align your awareness with catastrophe, Nature will factor those thoughts as your vote for the future. The peace movement can align itself with a healed planet, adding millions of votes to that side. And since our votes carry depth of awareness, they will be far stronger than any thoughtless vote for destruction.

Vision. When all the earlier elements are in place, vision goes on the move. Instead of languishing as an ideal that will never come true, a vision rooted in consciousness *must* come true. The proof of this always arises in hindsight. Columbus and Magellan were wrapped up in the particulars of putting together a long, arduous voyage at sea, with no assurance that they would succeed or even remain alive. Yet behind them, as we know now, was the pressure of collective consciousness. The Age of Exploration had gathered sufficient energy and will to become historical reality. This mesh of private vision and historical change is mysterious. We only remember the leading explorers and discoverers, but the intriguing part is how ordinary citizens got swept up by change.

The peace movement must take a further step, not just hoping to engage ordinary people but also knowing how that is done. These building blocks of consciousness are the only means we have, and fortunately they are the most powerful. We can leave the military stockpiles and the multinational corporations to whoever feels attached to them and therefore must defend them. Those emblems of the old order are nothing more than frozen consciousness. They may have power to affect everyday life, but the reins of change lie in our hands.

Anyone who knows how to move consciousness in an evolutionary direction is part of the peace movement. I find this immensely encouraging because there can't be a living human being whose makeup doesn't include at least a fraction of devotion to evolution. Our innate desire for more happiness ensures that this is true. Another portion of the self may believe that happiness will increase by building a new weapon, discovering a new technology of death, living in a country that is hugely militarized, and so forth. The old order is extensive and powerful; it has materialism on its side. Let that be as it may. The livelier part of awareness is always the leading edge, the part that wants to evolve. It takes time for the leading edge to convince the rest of the self to give up its old outworn habits, but the evolutionary impulse is irresistible.

The best thing you can do for peace today is encourage the evolutionary impulse in yourself. Developing peace consciousness is a practical project, and the more of us who engage in it every day, the more momentum we add to the future. The future doesn't exist in time; it isn't a place over the horizon of tomorrow. The future is the next shape that consciousness takes. A flower is the future of a seed. It takes time for the seed to turn into a flower, but in truth the pattern mapped out in the plant's genes controls time. It uses it to bring about a reality already deeply imprinted. Peace consciousness, once imprinted in our minds, can use time in exactly the same way, as the stage for an unfolding that was fully shaped in advance.

The peace movement will succeed as long as people can grasp small achievements every day. To that end, here is a program for peace you can implement here and now.

SEVEN PRACTICES FOR PEACE

How to become a peacemaker

THE PROGRAM FOR peace asks you to become a peacemaker by following a specific practice every day, each centered on the theme of making peace real, one step at a time, in your personal life.

Sunday: Being for Peace
Monday: Thinking for Peace
Tuesday: Feeling for Peace
Wednesday: Speaking for Peace
Thursday: Acting for Peace
Friday: Creating for Peace
Saturday: Sharing for Peace

Each practice takes only a few minutes. You can be as private or outspoken as you wish. But those around you will know that you are for peace by the way you conduct your life on a daily basis.

Sunday: Being for Peace

TODAY, TAKE FIVE minutes to meditate for peace. Sit quietly with your eyes closed. Put your attention on your heart and inwardly repeat these four words: *Peace, Harmony, Laughter, Love.* Allow these words to radiate from your heart's stillness out into your body.

As you end your meditation, say to yourself, *Today I will relinquish all resentments and grievances.* Bring into your mind a grievance against someone and let it go. Send that person your forgiveness.

Monday: Thinking for Peace

THINKING HAS POWER when it is backed by intention. Today, introduce the intention of peace in your thoughts. Take a few moments of silence, then repeat this ancient prayer:

> *Let me be loved, let me be happy, let me be peaceful.*
> *Let my friends be happy, loved, and peaceful.*
> *Let my perceived enemies be happy, loved, and peaceful.*
> *Let all beings be happy, loved, and peaceful.*
> *Let the whole world experience these things.*

If at any time during the day you are overshadowed by fear or anger, repeat these intentions. Use this prayer to get back to your center.

Tuesday: Feeling for Peace

THIS IS THE day to experience the emotions of peace. The emotions of peace are compassion, understanding, and love.

Compassion is the feeling of shared suffering. When you feel someone else's suffering, understanding is born.

Understanding is the knowledge that suffering is shared by everyone. When you understand that you aren't alone in your suffering, there is the birth of love.

When there is love there is the opportunity for peace.

As you practice, observe a stranger some time during your day. Silently say to yourself, *This person is just like me. Like me, this person has experienced joy and sorrow, despair and hope, fear and love. Like me, this person has people in his or her life who deeply care and love him or her. Like me, this person's life is impermanent and will one day end. This person's peace is as important as my peace. I want peace, harmony, laughter, and love in his or her life and the life of all beings.*

Wednesday: Speaking for Peace

TODAY, THE PURPOSE of speaking is to create happiness in the listener. Have this intention: Today every word I utter will be chosen consciously. I will refrain from complaints, condemnation, and criticism.

Your practice is to do at least one of the following:

Tell someone how much you appreciate him or her.

Express genuine gratitude to those who have helped and loved you.

Offer healing or nurturing words to someone who needs them.

Show respect to someone whose respect you value.

If you find that you are reacting negatively to anyone, in a way that isn't peaceful, refrain from speaking and keep silent. Wait to speak until you feel centered and calm, and then speak with respect.

Thursday: Acting for Peace

TODAY IS THE day to help someone in need: a child, a sick person, an older or frail person. Help can take many forms. Tell yourself, *Today I will bring a smile to a stranger's face. If someone acts in a hurtful way to me or someone else, I will respond with a gesture of loving kindness. I will send an anonymous gift to someone, however small. I will offer help without asking for gratitude or recognition.*

Friday: Creating for Peace

TODAY, COME UP with at least one creative idea to resolve a conflict, either in your personal life or your family circle or among friends. If you can, try and create an idea that applies to your community, the nation, or the whole world.

You may change an old habit that isn't working, look at someone a new way, offer words you never offered before, or think of an activity that brings people together in good feeling and laughter.

Second, invite a family member or friend to come up with one creative idea of this kind on his or her own. Creativity feels best when you are the one thinking up the new idea or approach. Make it known that you accept and enjoy creativity. Be loose and easy. Let the ideas flow and try out anything that has appeal. The purpose here is to bond, because only when you bond with others can there be mutual trust. When you trust, there is no need for hidden hostility and suspicion—the two great enemies of peace.

Saturday: Sharing for Peace

TODAY, SHARE YOUR practice of peacemaking with two people. Give them this text and invite them to begin the daily practice. As more of us participate in this sharing, our practice will expand into a critical mass.

Today, joyfully celebrate your own peace consciousness with at least one other peace-conscious person. Connect either through e-mail or by phone.

Share your experience of growing peace.

Share your gratitude that someone else is as serious about peace as you are.

Share your ideas for helping the world move closer to critical mass.

Do whatever you can, in small or large ways, to assist anyone who wants to become a peacemaker.

EFFORTS ARE UNDER way to bring this simple program to a worldwide audience. One can see that forming into communities of consciousness is easily possible. In the Internet age such communities don't have to be physical, although I can foresee that they will take that leap in the near future. A community of consciousness uses invisible building blocks to make a new reality. That is the bond that will unite us, no matter how far apart we live. The seven practices for peace are simple, but when followed on a mass scale, their power is potentially unlimited. If you transform yourself into a peacemaker, you won't become an activist marching in the streets. You will not be anti anything. No money is required. All you are asked to do is to go within and dedicate yourself to peace.

It just might work.

Even if you don't immediately see a decline in violence around the world, you will know in your heart that you have dedicated your own life to peace. The single best reason to become a peacemaker is that every other approach has failed. No one knows what the critical mass must be before peace becomes the foundation of a new order; your duty and mine is to bring about change by personal transformation. Isn't it worth a few moments of your day to end thirty wars around the world and perhaps every future war that is certain to break out? War is like cancer: it will only get worse if we don't treat it. Right now there are 21.3 million soldiers serving in armies around the world. Can't we recruit a peace brigade ten times larger?

A hundred times larger?

The project begins now, with you.

THE SPECTER OF THEM

T HE WAY OF peace teaches that no one is your enemy. Since this is such a radical change from the way we were taught to feel, it must happen by degrees. The first step is to stop believing in that legendary monster called *them*. Every enemy, when met face to face, turns out to be a human being. I recently read that on June 6, 1945, the day the Allies landed in Normandy, a disturbing phenomenon took place. It was discovered that the average G.I. wouldn't fire his gun at the Germans defending the beaches. Even under direct order, with a commanding officer marching down the line of riflemen and shouting the order to fire, only about one in twenty-five soldiers obeyed.

In the aftermath of war, when D-Day became a glorious victory for right and good, this unsettling fact was not made public. Only an internal U.S. Army report discussed it. In that report the reason for not firing was clear. It had nothing apparently to do with cowardice; rather, the G.I.s couldn't shoot advancing Germans because they saw them as human beings. From early childhood each rifleman had been taught that it was against God's law to kill, and that teaching was nearly impossible to overcome,

31

even in the heat of battle. This reluctance to fire on the enemy was a problem for the army, which decided to change its training methods. Instead of shooting and killing another human being, riflemen were taught to make contact with the target or fulfill the strategic objective. Which still means killing another human being, but with a thick mask of language papering over the brutal facts. The overall solution was to condition the average soldier never to see the enemy as fully human, certainly not as human as those fighting on our side.

Dehumanizing the other side isn't a modern invention. The peace movement today decries the fact that American warfare has turned into a high-tech video game. Soldiers can view the enemy on electronic screens that belong in arcades, and fire weapons at a great distance without ever seeing the face of those they destroy. Making the enemy less than human, however, is an age-old tactic, rooted in the notion of *them.*

THE RULES OF US VERSUS THEM

Beliefs that keep a false logic alive

It has to be us versus them.
They are evil, we are good.
We have to defeat them; otherwise they will destroy us.
They believe in a false God.
They are crazy.
They hate us and probably always will.
They deserve what they get.

If this logic sounds crude, I can only say that it would be impossible to exaggerate how cruelly such logic is actually used. A student of history can point to the British reaction to World War I.

Before 1914, the year of the war's outbreak, Germany occupied a place as a nation among nations, perhaps not an ally, but respected for its culture and philosophy. This same people, once the war began, turned into filthy Huns, accused of wanton torture, the wholesale murder of babies, and every fiendish crime imaginable. This demonization was considered a necessary part of the propaganda campaign to keep the public at a fever pitch for war.

WE SEE THE same demonization taking place now, for much the same reasons. Making *them* into creatures of evil is effective, as every war leader knows, but in the tangled hierarchy it isn't possible to segregate truth from fiction. Real atrocities are part of the mix, along with real horror and dismay at what happens in war. Partisanship adds its flavor, since the atrocities on our side get minimized and excused while those committed or even suspected by *them* get blown out of proportion.

Yet there is no doubt that to exploit fear is an act of cruelty. Ultimately the reason that *they* get turned into demons is so that more of *them* can be killed with a clear conscience. The cruelty is justified because of the end in sight, which is total victory. In a winning-is-everything ethos, the end must justify the means, since losing is a totally negative and therefore totally unacceptable outcome. This is true in competitive sports, where us-versus-them seems innocuous. But in war total victory is an illusion, unless you blank out the loss of life on the loser's side and discount the horrors of war that your soldiers endured to reach the moment of victory.

The way of peace calls for each person to abolish the logic of us-versus-them and to end one's allegiance to its rules. Each rule loses its grip on the mind when it is seen as false and unnecessary.

It has to be us versus them.

THE FIRST RULE is the most powerful and always has been. We can call it the root cause of conflict, because conflict demands separation. In spiritual terms, however, separation is the problem, not the answer. In us-versus-them thinking it is turned into the answer. If you can't get rid of people who are not like you, then why not fight them? Turn their otherness into your motivation. This is a delusion, for there is no alternative except to heal separation, to bring otherness to an end. If you accept the way of peace, your goal is always to heal, never to oppose. It isn't enough to say of radical Islamists that they are only somewhat bad. Although that sounds moderate and reasonable, such a position boils down to us-versus-them thinking in the end, for you are still condoning the war against their badness. The alternative is clear: work to end separation in your own life. Don't let easy judgments about how bad they are cloud the issue.

They are evil, we are good.

THIS RULE ADDS excitement and drama to the fight. Instead of facing the truth, which is that everyone is trapped in separation and needs to get out, we can fall back on the eternal war between good and evil. How exciting to realize that you have found someone to attack instead of seeing the enemy within yourself. The eternal war of light and darkness serves as easy cover. What makes it a sham is that this battle is never clear-cut. Life is always mixed, confusing, blended, and in turmoil. We are all in this together, no matter how enticing it is to load all the evil onto *them*.

We have to defeat them; otherwise they will destroy us.

THIS RULE TAKES the next step and turns *them* into aggressors. As a tactic of fear it is very effective. Evil, once labeled, never seems content to stay at home. It wants to spread; it wants to conquer and devour. The same logic holds for people who suffer from phobias. If you have a deep-seated fear of insects, for example, you imagine that they know you are afraid. Each grasshopper and spider isn't moving around randomly—it is heading for *you*. Phobics are intensely convinced by this logic, but standing outside the phobia, one sees immediately that it is irrational. Grasshoppers don't have a secret sense of who to get; in fact, they aren't out to get anybody, even though in their natural behavior they can prove destructive to crops, and so on.

Evil is rarely implacable. It can be incredibly stubborn, and in some cases (the classic one being Hitler) an entire society can fall prey to psychosis, mistaking good for evil. In families the abuser can gain such power that the other members forget that they are being harmed and instead side with him. But however stubborn evil can be, there is never a *they* who embody total evil and have only one mission in life, to seek out and destroy good.

They believe in a false God.

THIS RULE IS another way to bolster the status of virtue, by assuming that God likes war enough to choose sides. He chooses the side that truly knows him over the side that worships him falsely. Here, I think, is where the logic of us-versus-them loses its potency for many people. The teaching of an omnipotent God has sunk in too deep, and the notion of knowing what God wants is too uncertain. It makes no sense, when you think at all deeply about God, that he even needs defending in the first place. He is, after all, eternal, which means that he has existed an infinite span of time before this moment and will continue to exist for an infinite expanse of time afterward. How could he be threatened? The arguments that put God on one side of a war equally apply to the other side, and therefore the two cancel each other out. Unlike violence, the way of peace doesn't need God to justify it; it is justified by its own merits as a way to improve life for every person.

They are crazy.

THIS MAY SEEM like one of the crudest rules, but presently it has turned into one of the most appealing, even to sophisticated people. Radical Islamists in particular are held to be under the sway of bizarre thought processes. They reject the modern world and its technology. They refuse to see the obvious rightness of the capitalist West. They want to drag the world backward into some medieval age which was the last time they felt comfortable. Instead of being seen as contrary ideas, we view theirs as crazy, on a par with someone who might suggest the return of slavery or the subjugation of women (this idea enfolds itself into the crazy arguments against all of Islam rather easily).

What makes this argument so subversive is that you can tell yourself that committing violence against crazy people is for their own good. Unlike evil people, crazy people can't be held completely responsible for their acts. They are misguided and don't know it. Therefore we are justified in taking control of their lives away from them. But if you are killing people for their own good, the burden of irrationality may be falling more on your side than theirs.

They hate us and probably always will.

THIS RULE IS sheer projection, imagining how someone else feels because it serves how you want them to feel, or need them to feel. It is much easier on the conscience to hurt someone who hates you. But why should it be this way? If you hold a gun to someone's head and say, "I'm going to shoot you, but only if I can figure out your mood first," this rule is exposed for what it is, a way to pretend that violence is morally right because it feels right. Feelings and emotions don't change the immorality of violence. It's true that in some countries an accused killer can be let off on the basis that he committed a crime of passion, but in those cases the hatred wasn't in the victim but in the criminal. It's our hatred, not theirs, which blinds us. Making *them* the haters is a naked attempt to keep goodness on our side and to prevent the only process that will end violence: looking inward to discover one's own darker side.

They deserve what they get.

THIS RULE TOTALLY removes responsibility from the side committing violence and throws the whole burden onto the victim. In cases of domestic violence, it is commonly the abuser who complains that "she made me do it." The picture is one of a tolerant, resigned spouse who has been pushed too far and had no choice but to retaliate. Violent people can buy into this logic completely for their own psychological survival. (O. J. Simpson notoriously gave a press conference in which he described himself as the real victim of his marriage, despite and in the face of killing the other person.)

Blaming the victim is the most immoral and unwholesome form of us-versus-them logic. It reached a horrendous nadir when German SS officers who were assigned concentration camp duties bitterly complained that the Jews forced them to do what they did. This was actually a common complaint, and it arose because the duty of handling corpses and ashes on a mass scale was otherwise intolerable. Without the self-serving defense of blaming the victim, the job of the SS would have been seen as insanity, which is the truth. The way of peace is clear on this issue: No one deserves violation, and the acts of violence that you commit lie on your shoulders and nobody else's. *They* are never the excuse.

In the tangled hierarchy, victim and perpetrator are bound together. Ultimately there is no *them* because everyone is connected. We have to be willing to think at the level of collective consciousness—the awareness that makes us one humanity—as a daily way of thinking. Otherwise, the attraction of us-versus-them logic takes hold. Connections are tenuous at this stage. Disconnections are so prevalent that few people really see how harmful they are. How many times have you found yourself in any of the following positions?

Wanting your favorite sports team to crush their opponents
Backing a political candidate who uses smear advertising
Desperately wanting your company to get the competitive edge
Trying to look better than your neighbors
Praying to beat out a rival for a raise or a new job

In all these cases the tangled hierarchy brings many related ingredients into play: competitiveness, self-interest, ego, self-image, family image, town and national pride, anger, jealousy. Each context is unique, and yet all are the same. The individual begins to identify with some conflict. If the situation is too divisive, then there is no hope for healing the relationship between us versus them. Divisiveness is the fuel that keeps *them* in a degraded position. One's very self is defined by not being like *them.*

This is really the crux of the matter. The way of peace tells us that our true identity is at the level of spirit and nowhere else. All other identities are temporary. Many are simply false. Identity is subtle because it takes no thought. By osmosis you absorb one influence after another, until the voices in your head, the opinions you automatically spout, the list of likes and dislikes that are stored away in memory, all become second nature. It takes thought and intelligence to scrape away these encrusted judgments, for they are judgments born of choice. An infant may have no choice but to absorb influences as if by osmosis, out of the air, so to speak. But by a very early age we all formed a critical faculty; the choice-maker inside us has been a conscious mechanism ever since.

For me as an individual to be free, I have to confront myself with questions about who I really am, and this is done in large part by examining the layers of false identity that I mistakenly call me. The practical side of this process comes down to one very simple question that happens to grow a thousand arms, like a mental octopus.

Am I thinking for myself? Or am I thinking like:

A typical Indian.
A typical doctor.
A typical Californian.
A typical American.
A typical middle-aged male.
A typical person at my income level.

Like it or not, we are all typical. We attach some part of our identity to external groups and status. We identify with money and possession, success and failure. These are the outer layering of the false self, the typical reactions that I think are my own but really belong to a whole type of person.

It's tough at times, thanks to our cherished self-images, to believe that we are the product of cookie cutters. If you utter an opinion and someone reacts by muttering "typical," isn't that an insult? But watch yourself as you absorb information. Bombarded by thousands of pieces of news every day, your mind sorts it out lazily by latching on to those bits that already agree with your general makeup. If your general makeup, like mine, is that of a middle-aged Indian doctor living in a lush part of California, you will react to the news of race riots in New Delhi or a hurricane in Florida or rising malpractice settlements in a generic way. There will be a little wiggle room for your personal reaction, but frankly, not much. Unless you consciously divert your mind into new channels, it will react as predicted. News from India will make your mind perk up, hurricanes far away from home will spark little reaction, rising malpractice costs will cause anger and alarm.

The next layer of identity is more personal but just as illusory.

Am I thinking for myself? Or am I thinking like:

Everybody else in my family.
My parents when I was growing up.
My closest friends.
My intellectual equals.
Someone I love.

At this level the grip of false identity is more seductive. Isn't it a good thing to connect with those you love and respect? Of course, but it isn't good to absorb their ideas and opinions as if you thought them yourself, when in fact you chose these thoughts and opinions for ulterior motives: You wanted to be accepted. You wanted to be loved, or respected, or thought intelligent. One of my friends who travels in liberal circles called me to announce that he thought President Bush had done some good for himself with his acceptance speech at the 2004 Republican convention in New York.

"I didn't think much about having this reaction," he told me, "and I wasn't surprised that he got what they call a bump in the polls. But when I started to express my opinion, my friends really didn't like it. Some were angered, as if I was giving aid and comfort to the enemy. Some were repelled, as if I had said that Satan makes nice cupcakes. Some thought it just wasn't true, that I had made a quirky mistake.

"After a while, I noticed that I was a bit ashamed of my original reaction. I found myself apologizing for it. I offered reassurance, even when it wasn't asked for, that my loyalty hadn't changed. I threw in some gratuitous Bush-bashing so that everybody knew which side I was on. It wasn't a good reaction to have had, that much is clear."

In capsule form one sees here how insecure it feels to break out of one's normal identity. You no longer feel that you are on safe ground. People you count on may withdraw their friendship, love, and respect. Even the possibility of such a thing happening is terrifying to everyone at a certain level. We cling to false identity because it solves the problem of isolation. Rather than being alone and apart, we belong. But if we belong because of something as flimsy as opinion, what good is that belonging? How real is it?

Once you seriously ask, "Am I thinking for myself?" the

entire hierarchy of identity starts to unravel. If you keep asking without being daunted, eventually you get closer to the core. This is the final level of false identity.

Am I thinking for myself? Or am I thinking like:

The person I was yesterday.
The person I wish I could be.
An ideal image of myself.
A nobody trying to be a somebody.

How harsh the whole process of stripping away has become. It seems like suicide to go this deep, to the level where all you want is to be a somebody and not a nobody lost in a sea of bodies and faces. The paradox of separation is that it serves as both problem and solution. We put on these layers of false identity in order to be separate from everybody else, to feel unique and special. *I'm* not the vagrant asking for change on the street corner, *I'm* the businessman in a nice suit driving past that corner as fast as I can. *I'm* not the teenage Latino gang member being arrested for selling crack, *I'm* the upstanding citizen who pays taxes so that we can have a strong police force.

Yet at the same time we know that separation is the problem, which is why we worship those figures like Jesus who affirm that we aren't what we seem to be. Common humanity is beyond self-image. It's beyond the issue of whether you are a somebody or a nobody. If you follow the way of peace you don't try so desperately not to be a nobody. Those distinctions stop having power over you, because you turn into something different. Instead of a label, you become human. Instead of "I am X," you become "I am." The healing of separation is the beginning of true knowledge.

I must underline that this transformation isn't mystical. If I confront the first layer of false identity, I simply catch myself thinking like a type. I pay attention to my reactions when I start sounding too much like a typical Indian, a typical doctor, a typical middle-aged male. Having caught myself, I stop. Just that. I don't turn my opinions on top of their head. I don't strain to sound American, hip, young, populist, or anything else that would run counter to type. That would just be exchanging one set of types for another. Instead, I think to myself, "This isn't the real me." That single thought has tremendous power. It directly challenges the lazy mind, and it begins to ask it to think for itself.

I can then proceed a bit deeper. I catch myself whenever I am talking so that someone else will like me better. If my words are a disguised way of saying, Love me, accept me, respect me, I stop. There's nothing mystical in that act. Instead of talking, I listen. Instead of serving my own self-interest, I think about what everyone wants, or what is moral and good despite what everyone wants. Again, it all starts with the thought, This isn't the real me.

Finally, if I am thoroughly honest, I get to the deepest level. If I catch myself talking for the sake of my ego, I stop. This is more difficult, because the only alternative to self-importance is humility. The ego hates humility. There is softness in being humble. One feels unguarded, vulnerable. All those nobodies in the world might mistake you for one of them. So it takes a lot of negotiation with the self for this stage to progress. Day in and day out I will find myself falling back on the old strategies and tactics of the ego, the inflated, insecure, ever-vigilant part of everyone that wants to be important. But however long this negotiation may take (and it takes years), make no mistake—I have the trump card in my hand. I know that my self-image isn't the real me. And therefore what the ego sees as ultimate humiliation isn't any such thing. I am not becoming a nobody; I am becoming real.

Having taken the issue of us-versus-them to its spiritual core, I'd like to address the crudest level of this phenomenon, which has to do with terrorism. Terrorists are the new barbarians. Like Rome facing the hordes of invading Goths, modern Americans and Europeans feel that the threat of terrorism has come from beyond the frontier of civilization. A latter-day Roman would have hurled charges against the barbarians that sound grimly familiar. *They have no respect for life. They are without law. They harm the innocent without conscience. They are willing to die pointlessly. Their beliefs are beneath contempt.* Radical Islam is treated this way every day by our leading politicians, but not just by them. Intellectuals from both the right and the left repeat the same opinions—the only difference is that the left tends to utter them in sorrow and the right in anger.

What other attitude is there to take except sorrow or anger? The message seems to be that there is none, unless you are hopelessly sentimental or blind. The barbarians are coming, and they are perilously close to our walls. Those words echo a famous poem, "Waiting for the Barbarians," by the great Egyptian poet Constantine Cavafy. He imagines the day the Romans were waiting in dread for the arrival of the barbarian hordes from the north. The empire is already devastated. Only the final, fatal stroke remains. One feels an immediate tug to our own dread:

> *What are we waiting for, assembled in the forum?*
> *The barbarians are due here today.*
> *Why isn't anything happening in the senate?*
> *Why do the senators sit there without legislating?*
> *Because the barbarians are coming today.*
> *And when they come, they'll make their own laws.*

These are the perfect lines to have read the day after 9/11, when an entire society felt paralyzed by the approach of *them,* a people outside our notion of civilization. It was a moment when hope suffered one of its cruelest blows, although in sheer numbers Gettysburg or the Battle of the Somme, the killing fields of Cambodia or the machete uprising in Rwanda were far more horrific.

I feel myself standing there with Cavafy and the Romans. He describes how the emperor got up early so that he could sit in state when the barbarians crashed through the city's defenses. The wealth of Rome is also gathered there, equally helpless:

> *Why are they carrying elegant canes*
> *beautifully worked in silver and gold?*
>
> *Because the barbarians are coming today*
> *and things like that dazzle the barbarians.*

Cavafy tightens the strings of our nerves by painting no pictures of hurled spears, gashed skin, and screaming. There is only silent waiting and fear.

Then something bizarre happens. The crowd isn't getting the massacre they are poised to suffer. Restless and confused, they begin to disperse.

> *Because night has fallen and the barbarians have not come.*
> *And some who have just returned from the border*
> *say there are no barbarians any longer.*

Could this be true? Is it true for us, despite our paralyzing fear of *them*? Cavafy was thinking of his own time, during the era of Hitler and Mussolini, when he wrote these prophetic ending lines of the poem:

> *And now, what's going to happen to us without barbarians?*
> *They were, those people, a kind of solution.*

I think we have lived by that same solution for a very long time. The particular barbarians, whether Goths or Islamists, don't matter. In the perpetual existence of a single mind-set—us versus them—the hope for peace died.

What Cavafy so brilliantly realized is that if you eliminate the solution, the problem disappears. Both sides have to be tugging at their end of the rope to have a tug-of-war. If we let go of our end, the war ends. Who is coming over the horizon if not barbarians? Just more of the tangled hierarchy. Enemies who are also potential friends and allies. Angry emotions mixed with every other kind of emotion. In other words, the usual messiness. Yes, fierce opposition does exist, but so do layers of connection. Once, in a very worried moment, I turned to someone I barely knew in an airport and said, "What do you think those radical fundamentalists want? What are they about to do?" The stranger said, "I imagine they want what we want, to live a normal life with their kids." His saying that felt like cold water on my face, because my fear in the moment had made me forget the basic, undeniable fact that common life is pursued the same everywhere.

Terrorists have the power to suppress normal life and throw it into peril. I read a report from an American journalist embedded in Iraq who decided to venture out of the Green Zone, the safe areas of Baghdad controlled by the U.S. military. He went to a neighborhood mosque to talk with men as they emerged from prayer. The experience was striking, because he reports that ordinary Iraqis were moderate in their views. They expressed worry about the occupation. They wanted electricity and water to return as before. They expressed relief not to be living under a military dictatorship but anger that the occupying Americans had allowed thugs and insurgents to overrun the streets.

Then suddenly some hotheads joined the group around the reporter. They waved automatic rifles and began screaming and cursing. Instantly, the others in the group fell silent. The whole atmosphere changed, turning so violent that the reporter knew that his life might be in danger. The same men who a moment before had seemed like the voice of moderation now fell in with the extreme faction, adding their own shouts and curses.

In effect, this little drama was a lesson in identity. The tangled hierarchy isn't outside ourselves. We identify with a whole web of beliefs and influences. When there is pressure from one side, we identify with it; when there is pressure from another, our identity shifts. The group outside the mosque weren't giving in to evil; they were giving in to fear and anger, taking the course of least resistance by thinking in a typical way. The tangled hierarchy presented them a package they could possess in toto: Islam, its core beliefs, the ways of families and a society that has been telling itself stories for hundreds of years, the wishes of Allah, the Koran's laws and dictates. In a split second these men could identify with all of that, using no thought. The choices and beliefs were ready-made. You and I do the same thing whenever we fail to think for ourselves. Everyone is subject to losing the delicate thread of *I am* which is the only truth about identity, the only fact of the self that belongs to each of us without falsity.

Expanding this argument, the mentality of us versus them is always an expression of the root problem, which is dualism. Dualism is the belief that there are no final or absolute values, but only the play of opposites. In a dualistic world humans are separate from the source of creation. We are in its grip whenever we feel alone, isolated, and fearful of the world out there. Spiritual people are just as prone to this form of anxiety as nonspiritual people. They are prone to it for a different reason, however, because they devote themselves to fighting against duality all the time. Germs are always around the doctor who fights hardest against them. In Nietzsche's famous phrase, if you stare at a monster long enough, you become the monster. Which is a provocative way of saying that if you dwell on duality long enough, it swallows you up.

The solution, as I understand it, is to find a practical way to escape the divisions that duality imposes. These divisions run incredibly deep. Good versus evil. Dark versus light. Body versus soul. Us versus them. Even when you try with all your might to be on the side of the angels, the inescapable fact is that good defines evil and vice versa. The day that good was born it discovered that it had a twin in the cosmos, and both are immortal. The way of peace leads beyond duality. There is no other road to take for someone who wants to end war and violence. As Cavafy saw so clearly, there will always be a them as long as there is an us.

BEYOND TOXIC
NATIONALISM

DO WE LIVE in a country that stands for peace? Millions of Americans fervently believe they do, and ugly facts will not change their minds. They turn their backs on the damage America creates, almost thoughtlessly, around the world. American corporations that do not want to tolerate being regulated at home move overseas where they can pile asbestos in huge mounds that Asian children play on, sell potent pharmaceuticals over the counter in Thailand without the need of prescriptions, create a lethal gas leak in Bhopal, India, and generally damage the ecology in any way they choose. Being an American means all of those things. It's just as American to be the largest supplier of arms in the world and to send your troops into battle to be killed by these same arms. It's American to promote free markets whatever the cost, as one native culture after another is despoiled and corrupted by the dollar.

Henry James called it a complex fate to be an American, and it still is. I once heard someone say that we are the one country everyone hates and the one they all want to move to. Last year I saw a documentary on the free market system, which has basically become the new religion in American economics and conservative politics both. One economist after another praised our efforts to open up every foreign country to the American way of life. Free markets were credited with the end of Communism, the rescue of Chile from the iron grip of General Augusto Pinochet, and the general liberation of the world from stifling monopolies and class privilege.

In the midst of painting this rosy picture, the camera went to a street vendor in Thailand selling sandwiches from a cart. We followed this man as he left Bangkok and went north to the lush resort areas favored by Western tourists. He ended up at an eerie, ghostly place. It was a ruined hotel and golf course built on a grand scale. Walking through one half-constructed room after another, each now molding and tattered, the man made clear that he once owned this whole complex. He was a budding entrepreneur who had assembled millions of dollars to construct his dream.

The money came from a boom in Thai currency in the early 1990s, which was entirely created by American investors. A few money managers sitting at computers in New York sent the Thai economy into a dizzying rise. None had ever been to Thailand or knew anybody who lived there. Then just as precipitously they became nervous about the Asian currency market, and almost overnight the boom reversed itself into a catastrophic plunge, and a man who on Monday was building a dream resort found himself on Tuesday selling sandwiches from a street stand. The double face of America as the world's best friend and worst enemy was starkly revealed to me.

In the past, dealing with such ugly facts wasn't necessary. You could simply shield yourself from them, as many people do now. One road to the future will turn the U.S. into a fortress, isolated against the realities outside its borders. In that future we will

ignore the disparity between rich and poor that has already created so much harm. America possesses around five percent of the
world's population but consumes about a third of its natural
resources. We emit half of the greenhouse gases like carbon diox-
ide that are linked to global warming. Yet in fortress America
none of that will count as much as remaining comfortable and
rich.

The other road to the future leads to globalization. America
will dedicate itself to everything that is being ignored at the present moment. It will become a leader in reversing global warming,
protecting other economies, closing the gap between rich and
poor nations, and ending the devastating pandemic of AIDS.
(It's stunning to realize that a mere fraction of the U.S. defense
budget would be enough to treat every person in Africa infected
with HIV. The same infected Africans could be treated for a
month for the cost of a single Stealth bomber.) For any of this to
happen, however, our brand of nationalism would have to stop
being toxic and begin to be healing.

The way of peace is dedicated to the second alternative. If
the future is fortress America, peace has no real chance. For
once, the tangled hierarchy leads to a clear choice. To keep going
in the direction of toxic nationalism is a recipe for disaster. I
realize that to the rest of the world globalization may no longer
be seen as a virtuous alternative for America; it is condemned as a
cloak for American dominance. But America must reach out and
become part of the globe in a positive way. This has become so
clear over the last decade that most people, I believe, see the writing on the wall. America must globalize or go down with the
planetary ship.

My activist friends, who grumble darkly about the doomed
American empire and its policy of economic apartheid, grow
angrier by the day. Why do we keep making such tragically wrong

choices? they ask. Why do we remain in the grip of unreality when the problems facing us are so obvious and urgent? Sometimes these are rhetorical questions, but if one asks them seriously, the answer lies in the power of nationalism itself.

America is an identity. When you say "I am American" you are not just stating a simple label. You are giving someone your history. You are implying certain values, and since America has a tradition of democracy and liberty, it is easy for politicians to play up any criticism of America as an attack on our identity. By this twisted logic it becomes un-American to want anything good for the world if it involves changing our way of life.

When the word *un-American* entered common usage during the communist scare of the early 1950s, few people asked if the term even made sense. Take two things that are opposite: being for war and being for peace. Which one is American and which one un-American? They can't be both at the same time, yet as the national mood shifts, one or the other is considered so un-American that you have to be fast on your feet to keep up with the right way to think.

The deeper question is not about being American or un-American—it's whether nationalism itself keeps wars going. The ethos of pumped-up patriotism that surrounds daily life right now has put so much pressure on people to conform that one forgets how lowly nationalism used to be regarded. Albert Einstein was scornful on the subject: "Nationalism is an infantile disease. It's the measles of humanity." The noted psychologist Erich Fromm was abrupt and clinically cold: "Nationalism is our form of incest. It is our idolatry, and patriotism is its cult." But many observers during the era of National Socialism in Germany had lived through one virulent outbreak of violence after another in the name of the fatherland or motherland. Many commentators were quick to pick up the theme that nationalism is a disease.

Even though I find few condemnations of nationalism in the current news, there is a detectable undercurrent of doubt. This book depends upon the possibility that many people have become internal defectors, so to speak, able to question the whole notion that a good country is one that turns to armed violence and intimidation as an automatic reflex. The way of peace isn't anti-American, a fact I feel needs to be stated. As a people, Americans feel that they are good and loving, as indeed we are. But a lack of awareness has caused good, loving people to believe in half-truths and falsehoods, as in the following:

Ours is the freest country in the world. This claim, the bedrock of Americanism, is an emotional outcry, not a reality. The citizens of every Western European country are just as free as we are and have been since the end of World War II.

This country stands for equality. In principle we do, but about one percent of Americans in the upper income brackets control ninety percent of the wealth. The fastest-growing sector of the economy is in low-paying jobs like building services (jargon for janitors and cleaning women) and restaurants.

We are a beacon of democracy for the rest of the world. Another emotional statement, and an idealistic one. Voter turnout in our democracy is among the lowest in any country, advanced or developing. Many commentators have direly noted that the enormous influence of lobbyists and special interests far outstrips the influence of ordinary citizens in having their wishes enacted into law. The U.S. Senate is overwhelmingly a body of rich white males, a sizable proportion of whom are lawyers. Democracy depends upon fair representation in government, yet if you happen to be black, Hispanic, or a woman, your interests are represented very meagerly in Congress.

America is the melting pot of the world. As an immigrant, I took advantage of America's openness, and there is no doubt, despite the current suspicion of immigrants and new rules clamping down on them, that America is the land of opportunity. However, to many immigrants this means economic opportunity only. The value of American citizenship is chiefly measured in money and comfort. Many historians have also pointed out that far from being a melting pot, America has a tradition of warring ethnic factions (think of the street battles between Irish and Italians in Boston and New York that flourished around the Civil War and persisted, as simmering animosity, until recent memory).

Some minorities segregate themselves in order not to melt into a single national identity, as witness the move for bilingual (i.e., Spanish) education and the growth of private schools for Muslims that concentrate heavily on the Koran as the authority on government and citizenship. Other minorities, especially blacks, are caught between voluntary segregation in their own communities and feeling forced by racism to live apart. The tangled hierarchy must always be kept in mind, because one oppressed minority may be racist against another. Consider, for example, the hostility that black ghetto residents have shown toward Jewish and Korean store owners. In many urban areas, their businesses are sure to be among the first ones attacked and looted during any racial disturbance.

America is the peacekeeper of the world. This piece of national rhetoric seems unassailable to most Americans. The rest of the world is not so sure. Sympathy for this country reached a high after 9/11, when sixty-seven percent of those polled overseas said that they approved of America. Old allies from World War II went out of their way to mention their lasting gratitude for the U.S. coming to rescue them from fascism. But today foreign polls show that only twenty-seven percent of their citizens approve of America, due to the invasion of Iraq; and this percentage is much lower in Arab countries. More shocking to our national self-image was the response to another question: Which country do you think poses the greatest danger in the world? While seven percent of respondents picked North Korea, one of the triad singled out by President Bush in the axis of evil, eighty-five percent picked the United States.

Reciting these unsettling facts about the U.S. is sure to arouse visceral anger in some people. The way of peace asks us to look at how we automatically identify with the nation, blending "America" and "me" as if they are fused. Krishnamurti was making a psychologically valid point when he said that nationalism is sophisticated tribalism. It is even more potent than that. One of the most startling turns of events in Iraq was the unity shown by Sunnis and Shiites. It may turn out that by the time you read this Iraq will have broken out in a religious civil war of Sunni versus Shia, but right now they are united under the old adage of "the enemy of my enemy is my friend." Both sides hate America enough to forget how much they hate each other.

What brought these two foes together was nationalism. A virulent Iraqi nationalism had been fostered for decades by Saddam Hussein's regime. It fueled the attacks on Iran in the 1980s and Kuwait in the 1990s. Although our own patriots would be incensed at comparisons between American nationalism and Iraqi nationalism, the same ingredients are always present in the tangled hierarchy:

pride
tradition
attitude of superiority
patriotism
national security
military buildup
defensiveness

armed borders

enemies real and imagined

I am not equating the two countries here at all—one nation's particular mix of these ingredients will be different from another's. But many of us find it humiliating to America's self-image that the more disturbing aspects of nationalism, such as putting assault weapons in the hands of ordinary citizens, mounting quasi-illegal militias, and allowing religious venom to flavor the national debate, are endemic to both U.S. and Iraqi society. People would like to believe that there is a big difference between nice nationalism (our kind) and nasty nationalism (their kind), but the disease itself is the real problem.

Keeping the populace in a state of defensive resentment against the West, and especially the U.S., was a constant under Saddam Hussein. He oversaw the oppression by force of the Shiite majority, which outnumbered the ruling Sunnis by more than two to one. Hussein was modern in that he had advanced beyond religion. He was canny enough to exploit those feelings, too. When he invaded Kuwait in 1990, mobs of black-veiled Iraqi women appeared in the streets shouting their approval of a good Islamic man who would teach a lesson to the decadent, over-Westernized Kuwaiti women. That the war had much more cynical roots, having to do with excessive oil surpluses and the large debt Iraq owed to Kuwait's banks, was well cloaked.

Charges that the Bush administration is just as cynically making use of the Iraqi conflict and that it is all about the oil are rife right now. History will make its own judgments. You and I must keep in mind that even without cynicism, nationalism is a false way to view reality, and breaking through its illusions is crucial to the way of peace.

ENDING AN ILLUSION

The toxic effects of nationalism

The illusion is that nationalism helps to free people.
The reality is that nationalism is now the same as militarism.

The illusion is that other nations are inferior, misguided, and
wrong in their ways.
The reality is that every nation struggles with inner conflicts.

The illusion is that God favors one country and supports its
destiny.
The reality is that God has never expressed an opinion about
any nation, and never will.

The illusion is that national boundaries make us secure.
The reality is that we live in an open world where boundaries
mean less and less.

The illusion is that your country defines who you are.
The reality is that finding out who you are requires self-
searching and self-knowledge.

EACH OF THESE pairs shows a way for consciousness to grow by
facing reality. Every illusion was once true, or at least had the
weight of truth on its side. But consciousness is always on the
move. Liberating ideas turn into shackles unless we change them.
The first pair, for example, concerns freedom. After the American and French revolutions, nationalism was the rallying cry for

freedom at a time when the alternatives were much worse. One worse alternative was to fall under the power of colonialism, as India, China, and all of Africa had. Another was to be an oppressed province of an empire, as Italy, Greece, and most of the Middle East were, or an ethnic minority, as many of the former republics of the Soviet Union were. In rebellion against these conditions, people wanted political freedom, and becoming a nation gave them a chance to achieve that.

But the situation has shifted, and nationalism today is a form of oppression known as militarism. To live in a society dominated by the military is the opposite of being free. The rhetoric of freedom prevails in post-colonial regions of Africa, which won their freedom beginning in the 1950s with the turbulence in Kenya and the Belgian Congo. Today, there are barely a handful of countries in Africa that are not armed military dictatorships.

But the most pernicious illusion is that your country defines who you are. We are constantly told that America is now a bitterly divided nation, with the mindless implication that if we all just remember how American we are, the rift would heal. The "red" and "blue" states stand for cultural opposites, on the one side predominantly rural, conservative, and fundamentalist in religious belief, on the other side predominantly urban, moderate, and liberal in religious belief. This division doesn't actually hold true, in the sense that there is a sharp line in values and concerns. Most people feel confused about hot issues but take a stand because in confusing times ambiguity isn't tolerated. Changing your mind is condemned as showing weakness, even though it could be characterized as a sign that you are intelligent enough to realize that every issue has more than one side. The political process doesn't allow you to cast three-quarters of a vote even if you only agree with seventy-five percent of a candidate's positions, so the pressure to be pro or con is strong.

"Liberal" and "conservative" are muddy terms now. A person who reluctantly votes for the Iraq war is immediately put in the same camp with vociferous hawks. Taking a stand on any hot issue like abortion or prayer in the schools shouldn't be a test of character. We find ourselves projecting values onto others that they don't actually hold.

It's possible to create a total picture of another person with no real information at all. A fascinating experiment conducted at Harvard in the 1960s turned on this fact. Each subject was invited into a room and seated before a panel that had two buttons on it. This experiment, they were told, is a study in gamesmanship. On the other side of this wall is another player who also has two buttons. If he presses button #2 and you press button #1, he gets two dollars and you get nothing. If you press button #2 and he presses button #1, you get two dollars and he gets nothing. If you both press button #2, you each get nothing. But if you both press button #1, you each get a dollar.

The subjects quickly absorbed what was at stake. If they got greedy and kept pressing button #2, their partners could retaliate by doing the same thing, and the net result would be no money for either side. But if they silently agreed to keep pressing button #1 without cheating to snatch an extra dollar here and there, they would be able to get more money for themselves without hurting the other person.

Most subjects figured this out after a few tries at pushing button #2 and finding that their partners did the same thing. Greed gave way to cooperation, and most people began to push #1. At the end of the session they were asked to give a description of what kind of person their partner was, based entirely on how he had played the game.

Consistently the descriptions were harsh. *This guy is selfish and stupid. This guy only wanted to play for himself. He's a bastard.* The same words tended to be repeated: irrational, stubborn, sneaky, under-handed, treacherous, greedy. For hard as they tried to send a sig-nal of being willing to push #1, the subjects found that the player on the other side of the wall kept pushing #2 at random moments. What they didn't know was that there was no partner on the other side of the wall, only a machine generating a ran-dom string of ones and twos.

Anything the subject thought he knew about his partner was complete projection. In fact this was an experiment in pure pro-jection, not gamesmanship or cooperation at all. We are so used to passing judgment on others that politicians can count on it. Keeping the people of other nations behind a screen makes it easy to label them with whatever emotion you wish to project. I read that the biggest laughs from the floor of the 2004 Republi-can National Convention came when any speaker used the words *France* or *French*. The knee-jerk reflex of derision could be counted on since the French have been characterized in the press as foot-dragging, uncooperative, antagonistic to war even when justified, anti-American, self-centered, and apparently against freedom itself (to judge by the decision in the Congressional cafeteria to rename French fries as "freedom fries").

In reality the French had turned out to be right on the facts. They were skeptical of the existence of weapons of mass destruc-tion in Iraq. They predicted that the Middle East would be in-flamed by an attack on Saddam Hussein, with the real possibility that terrorism would be encouraged rather than suppressed. They didn't believe that Saddam Hussein posed an immediate threat to other countries, and in general they felt that war should be a last resort. But the facts did the French little good. Once they were put behind the screen and became *the other*, they were fair game for any projection that fervent pro-war groups wanted to make.

Most of us have lived through a time when projection nearly tore this country apart. The Vietnam War created an enormous breakdown of the old story about America. Since war is without a doubt the very worst way to create change, I'd like to recall Vietnam protest as an example of the same upheaval we now face. The decade of the 1960s won't repeat itself, but its tangles and confusion already have.

I came to the U.S. in 1970 as a young medical intern in Plainfield, New Jersey. On my first night in the ER I took care of the first gunshot victims I'd ever seen. I would treat hundreds more as the everyday fact of American violence sank in. But not far from the center of my vision was Vietnam. The next year, 1971, saw the biggest mass protests for peace in American history. That year's March on Washington was especially rancorous because of Nixon's invasion of Cambodia and the Kent State killings the year before.

I learned more sharply than ever how intertwined peace and violence are. These protests were theaters of rage and resistance on both sides. Washington was armed to the teeth, its standard reaction to mass protest since 1967, with army sharpshooters mounted on the rooftops of government buildings and a huge presence of police backed by National Guardsmen in the wings in case things really got out of hand. On May 2, 1971, the police arrested 7,000 demonstrators in one day, mostly on the flimsy pretext of drug possession. This was the largest mass arrest in the country's history.

Seventy-five clergymen had been enlisted to calm the crowds, but the authorities were clearly in command. The D.C. police had learned how to perfect quickie mass arrests. Instead of the traditional process, which involved the arresting officer writing out a detailed report on the reason for the arrest, short forms with fill-in-the-blank entries were drawn up. In place of metal handcuffs, cheap flexible plastic ties were handed out by the thousands. A policeman is expected to present a plausible case in court, an obvious impossibility when you are arresting so many people at once. So Polaroid cameras were set up beside each paddy wagon, allowing the police to be photographed next to the accused. This photo would serve as a memory aid in case a judge wanted to know what a particular person had done.

All this efficiency eventually went by the boards. The D.C. police scooped up too many protestors to bother with formalities, and since the city's jails couldn't hold all the arrested, they were herded outside into holding pens. The protestors never succeeded in their avowed aim to shut Washington down for a day as a symbol of anti-war fervor. Yet this victory by the Establishment didn't erase the bitter truth that peace had become a mini-civil war.

The Vietnam peace movement is a perfect example of why our present condition is so confusing. Values were in flux; people wildly projected onto each other. The tangled hierarchy was dominated by new concepts that the old story of America couldn't assimilate:

hippie
protestor
flower child
generation gap
anti-Establishment
military-industrial complex
hawks
doves
domino effect
extremism in the defense of liberty

The Summer of Love was only four years old by 1971, but the protests had already gone through a dizzy evolution beyond love and flower children. One reads of hippie girls in the October 1967 March on the Pentagon dancing in front of soldiers with bayonets saying "Will you take my flower? Are you afraid of flowers?" Racial injustice became part of the protest, non-violence was polluted by the terrorist tactics of the Weather Underground who bombed college laboratories linked to the defense department, and people who opposed the war were branded as traitors.

Motives never remain pure in the tangled hierarchy. Opposites infect each other. Good intentions become blurred and compromised. The peace movement from that era was very sure of its moral position, yet in hindsight a great many Americans blame the protestors for losing the war, shaming the country, bringing divisiveness and conflict out into the streets, and creating general turmoil. It was a time of rising consciousness, yet also a time when crime rates tripled, never to return to their former levels, and drug use increased a thousandfold.

No society emerges from war intact. This held true for Vietnam as it did for World War II and World War I before it. The same is inescapable now. The ongoing conflict in the Russian republic of Chechnya is a prime example of how single-minded patriotism becomes a form of self-destruction. As I write this paragraph, terrorists fighting for a free Chechnya have occupied a school in the city of Beslan in southern Russia. They broke in with bombs and guns on one of the most cheerful days of the year, the first day of school, which is a holiday in Russia. In a catastrophic rescue attempt, the Russian military, together with the exploding bombs of the terrorists, caused the death of hundreds of hostages, including more than 175 children.

This news will have already reached you, and you will have felt the sick sorrow of knowing that terrorism has crossed yet another line, drawing in masses of innocent children. Today I read of a mass rally against terrorism in the heart of Red Square in Moscow. The mayor of the city shouted into the microphone, "Muscovites! We are not weak. We are stronger than them! Stronger! The fascists couldn't beat Russia and terror won't beat Russia either. We are together. We are going to win!"

The outside world finds it hard to comprehend why Russia is willing to undergo a bloody struggle to keep hold of a remote republic in the Caucasus after it willingly dissolved most of the former Soviet Union. President Vladimir Putin has latched on to the grim specter of Islamic fundamentalism, merging his fight against a free Chechnya with the global war against Osama bin Laden and his followers. This has become a self-fulfilling prophecy: now the leading Chechen rebel, Shamil Basayev, a fiercely bearded fighter with a shaved head who formerly fought beside the Russians, models himself as a charismatic terrorist in the bin Laden mold and calls upon Al-Qaida as his tactical allies.

If you and I feel anguish and revulsion at the Beslan attack, we may turn our heads while Russia does what it needs to do to fight back; already Putin is calling for increased powers on an unprecedented scale. But what we should do instead is look directly at the tangled hierarchy, for this is by no means a clear case of black and white. To prevent Chechnya from declaring independence, the Russians invaded the region in 1994. The capital city of Grozny was reduced to rubble and is now a bleak and totally lawless landscape reminiscent of Berlin after World War II. Eighty thousand Chechens, almost all of them civilians, were killed, and many more were left homeless.

The tangled hierarchy leaves no strand untouched. Here we have toxic nationalism on both sides, given that both resort to atrocity. We have complex ties to Islam and the romance of the jihad, counterbalanced by the old Soviet state, whose legacy of repression against religion still hangs heavy over the whole country. When you look directly at this tangle, the urge to take sides becomes less compelling, even though we can still feel emotionally pulled as events unfold. The only solution is to untangle the hierarchy. In this case the first step is to move past the illusions of nationalism.

But what would we put in its place?

Nationalism can't be changed by direct confrontation. Putting any country into a defensive posture increases the level of violence tenfold. That realization lies behind a famous remark from Mother Teresa: "People ask me why I don't join in the anti-war movement, and I say, I will join when you can show me a pro-peace movement." In that spirit, the current peace movement is beginning to find a way to befriend all nations by addressing the global need to end violence regardless of how one might feel about this regime or that, this ideology or that, this religion or that. These new peace groups are often pioneers in the application of technologies that mainstream society considers unbelievable. But as one remarkable hands-on healer once told me, anyone can heal; the chief obstacle is that you believe you can't.

"I went to this party," a young woman friend told me, "and we were bending spoons for world peace. I know, it sounds laughable when you first hear about it. There's a course I took on the Internet. The idea was, If we can use the technology of prayer to bend a spoon with our minds, maybe we can also bend the whole world toward peace.

"They said that anyone could learn to bend a spoon in less than four weeks. You make a donation and take the course, which centers on prayer, focused attention, and imaging. You open up parts of your consciousness that are blocked right now. There's no forcing with the mind. They said that for the technique to work, you have to see the spoon as already bent. I got together with other people at someone's house. It was amazing to see that some people got it very quickly. Now I've seen spoon-bending with my own eyes, and I think I'm getting close."

The logic here is very clear: if you can prove to yourself that you have the ability to break through the veil of ordinary reality, you can go on to do things that once seemed impossible or magical. The most prominent person in the spoon-bending movement, James Twyman, goes to troubled spots around the world to lead prayer vigils for peace, and his experience is that these Great Experiments change reality immediately. On February 9, 2004, his vigil was held in Jerusalem. It included participants from the Web as well as those physically present, and the next day violence on the West Bank fell by fifty percent or more. This result echoes earlier experiments by other spiritual groups. A popular Buddhist movement in Japan has put a prayer shield over that country to protect it since the mid-1960s. Round-the-clock prayer vigils are a regular part of sequestered life among some Catholic monasteries and convents. For more than a decade the Transcendental Meditation movement (TM) has been gathering large groups of meditators in cities like New York and Washington, then using police data to show that crime rates drop dramatically during those periods. The effect of these experiments may be lasting and not just a fleeting blip in the statistics of violence. TM and other consciousness groups believe that they have changed the trend of the future. Talk of creating a shift in the global brain isn't new, having circulated for thirty years now.

It seems to me that whether you are one of Twyman's Spiritual Warriors jetting off for a vigil in Jerusalem or someone who meditates privately at home, the influence for peace is real. One shouldn't be distracted by debunkers and skeptics who offer trivial tricks from the magician's bag to explain away very interesting phenomena. The debunkers won't stop despite the fact that hundreds of people attest to bending spoons or keys with their minds. I was present at a demonstration in Oxford, England, where more than 200 people, mostly from the university community, participated by holding up a key and attempting to bend it. About ten or twenty percent succeeded on their first try.

On the other side, it probably doesn't help to ease skepticism when spoon-benders dwell on the so-called mysteries and secrets surrounding what they do. The bald truth is this: consciousness determines which phenomena are real and which aren't. Every act of magic is actually the result of giving permission for a hidden natural law to come to the surface, emerging from its cave of darkness where we have forced it to hide.

Jet propulsion was a hidden magic for thousands of years, just as much as moving objects with thought (telekinesis) is now. Seeing a plane take off isn't magical to us anymore, but seeing a person levitate would be. The difference may be nothing more than acceptance. The average person cannot tell you how a vehicle made of steel weighing a hundred tons can fly, but as long as someone else can, the technology of flight is allowed to enter human awareness as a real thing and no longer a mystery.

If someone can explain how the technology of world peace works, that too will be allowed to exist as a reality. I think the impossibility of peace lies only in our heads, and once we begin to accept the impossible, a rapid shift will occur. In the meantime, I am grateful for stories like the following, from one of the spoon-bending participants: "Some friends of ours have a twelve-year-old son. We were talking about the spoon-bending course one night after dinner. As we were talking, their son decided to see if he could bend one of his mother's heavy-duty nice silver spoons. And he did! It bent in a weird way—not at a natural thin place. It actually freaked him out to be face to face with a reality that his culture tries to deny."

We cling to a reality that defines magic as a fraud, fantasy, or superstition. Whether it is telekinesis, healing, clairvoyance, or any number of openings, all kinds of phenomena give a peek behind the mask of materialism. From that point on, spiritual doubts that were plausible begin to vanish. Random events begin to form patterns. You realize that the creator who got lost in his creation is you. The truth dawns when you start to find out who you really are, disposing of all false labels. The deeper problem with nationalism isn't that it has become toxic but that it has hijacked part of our identity, and like every other part we have surrendered, this one must be reclaimed.

THE MYTH OF SECURITY

THE MAN ON television looked worried. In part this was because, being a serious commentator, he was paid to. But he also looked like someone who had just absorbed a deeply troubling truth.

"Half the people in the world live on two dollars a day," he said. "That's according to the best estimate of the World Bank. Most of those people living on two dollars a day know that we are rich. About twenty percent of the world's population live on one dollar a day. They also know that we are rich. Maybe fifty years ago they didn't, but now they do."

His tone grew more grave. "It used to be that it took vast armies to wield weapons of mass destruction. But now these weapons have been miniaturized. So one person or a small group walking down any city street can wield a weapon of mass destruction."

He stopped, not wanting to spell out doom. Billions of people living in stifling poverty are aware that a few hundred million live in wealth. Weapons of indescribable danger are potentially available to any of these people.

What will the result be?

Your mind can go one way and begin to multiply the potential for havoc. Like bacteria that have found a fertile host, fear can keep doubling upon itself. The attack of 9/11 spawned future attacks in our imagination, not just one more but potentially a multitude—couldn't they blow up any bridge, poison any water supply they wanted to? But your mind doesn't have to move that way. It can move toward understanding, which says that we have to adapt to a new way of being in the world if we expect to ever feel secure again. Once more the tangled hierarchy must be confronted. The key words in this particular hierarchy are especially intimidating because we have been told, over and over, how necessary they are to our very existence. The key terms include:

military
defense
multinational corporations
profits
shareholders
secret contracts
secret budgets
classified information
lobbyists
influence
nationalism

Touch any one of these threads and you quickly find that some group has something they desperately want to protect. If it's not the military itself, it's the defense contractors who depend upon them, the communities where defense plants provide the bulk of the jobs, the frightened public that wants to feel secure from attack, the lobbyists whose future depends upon the influence they can peddle, and so on through most of society. Nobody is more than a few degrees of separation away from this tangled hierarchy. A war-protesting student at Harvard is embedded in a university whose enormous wealth is directly linked to defense spending and government grants.

Even in developing countries, the balance between weapons and human services is totally skewed. Countries choose to embrace the hierarchy of war when it is clearly in their interest not to. South Africa was exposed to sharp criticism when it was discovered that the country was preparing to buy a nuclear submarine despite the fact that the government could find almost no money to fund AIDS awareness programs. This in a country that has not the slightest need for a nuclear submarine costing hundreds of millions of dollars but does have one of the worst AIDS crises in the world.

Does one need to mention that this same South Africa gave birth to Nelson Mandela, an icon of peace? But then India, the home of Mahatma Gandhi, has one of the largest standing armies in the world, just behind the United States, Russia, and China. Most of the world's largest defense budgets (as compared to total GNP) are found in poor developing countries. Swords instead of bread is the rule, not the exception.

The monster of arms dealing keeps growing because each of us, though not in the business, depends upon its hierarchy. It's not the venal acts of evil-doers that doom us but the drab facts of commerce and the fight for survival in a capital-driven world. Individual programs like the Strategic Defense Initiative (SDI), popularly known as Star Wars, have already cost more than the gross national product of a typical country in Africa or South America, despite the fact that SDI's purpose—to put a shield into space against invading Soviet nuclear missiles—is grossly outdated.

SDI is a particularly surreal project considering that shooting down guided missiles has never worked except in the most rudimentary tests with dummy rockets whose position and trajectory were known in advance. (It's satirically rumored that President Ronald Reagan was attracted to Star Wars because the technology mimicked a sci-fi B movie that he had starred in during his acting career in the 1930s.) Even if technologically perfected, the system would be totally useless against the real present threat, which is stateless terrorism. But surrealism aside, turning to weapons already in use, a single Stealth B-2 bomber costs an estimated $2.4 billion dollars, enough to fund every symphony orchestra and museum in the country. Arms outstripped culture long ago.

As with any monster, you must find its most vulnerable spot to defeat it. The hierarchy of weapons depends on three core beliefs. The whole culture of armaments would end if these beliefs no longer entangled us. In a materialistic world they have far more power over people than traditional religious morality, which has always been on the side of peace, but to less and less effect.

MYTHS ABOUT SECURITY

Core beliefs behind the arms buildup

Money brings happiness.
Technology brings well-being.
Military strength brings security.

No matter how isolated you feel from the business of making war, you are tied to it through relationships that begin here. You may feel moral outrage at the excesses of the arms industry and its potential for even grosser acts of inhumanity. (I read recently about a proposed technology which would allow heat-seeking neutron bombs to find people by body temperature and then vaporize them on contact. This grotesque invention, if it ever comes to pass, will solve the problem of wasting valuable buildings and bridges and other structures that get needlessly destroyed in war.) However, your moral outrage has little power to change a hierarchy that you are supporting by your very way of life. Consciously or not, you are worshipping these new gods, and their material hold over you and everyone else is the problem, not whether God is pleased or displeased by your country's defense policies.

Money and Happiness

I HAVE NEVER accepted that money was the root of all evil. Yet the way of peace has to face the current dominance of greed. Some liberal Christian theologians have tried to soften Christ's apparently blanket condemnation of riches by saying that what he really meant was that love of money is at the root of all evil. The semantic difference is that in the first statement money causes evil while in the second it is only associated with it. (The gun lobby makes the same semantic distinction when it declares that guns don't kill, people do. The guns just happen to be there a great deal of the time.) We have no completely reliable authority to tell us what Christ actually taught, but there's no doubt that every spiritual tradition tends to split apart the sacred and material realm.

The issue of money and spirituality has changed since Saint Francis of Assisi formed a band of impoverished brothers, recognized by the Pope in 1210 as the Franciscan order. Saint

Francis took literally a Biblical passage in which Christ says to his disciples, "You have received the Gospel without payment, give it to others as freely. Take no gold, or silver, or copper in your belts, no bag for your journey, no spare garment, nor sandals, nor staff." Begging monks were a tradition that was already centuries old in India and China. In a modern society money is still suspected to be a sign of unworthiness before God, and the wandering monks I saw in my childhood in New Delhi have disappeared from the streets today, a sign of the rampant materialism that India is embracing in imitation of the West.

The basic problem with money seems obvious: it pulls the mind toward worldly things, it fills up one's hours with business and commerce, it distorts the true values of spirit by replacing them with pleasure and possessions. To me, this doesn't say that money is evil or nonspiritual. It says that money is a distraction, and sometimes so powerful a distraction that people fail to go beyond it. The failure here is to unite spiritual and material values, but I believe the way of peace shows us that this is not only desirable but totally necessary.

It's fascinating that before he became Saint Francis, the young Francesco Bernardo was pulled toward a military life, which he saw as an avenue to greatness. He was captured in battle against the state of Perugia and held captive for a year. During this time he fell seriously ill and formed doubts about his military career, but on returning home to Assisi, he soon turned his ambitions back to the military. On a second campaign to the Neapolitan states he again fell seriously ill, but by this time the saint-to-be was having visions and hearing divine voices that were moving him in another direction. Several more decisive events took place. He encountered a leper while riding on horseback; he dismounted and embraced the cripple, then gave him all the money in his purse. He made a pilgrimage to Rome, where his sympathy was stirred by the beggars gathered at the door of Saint Peter's basilica. Francis exchanged his rich merchant's clothing with one of the beggars and spent the rest of the day fasting in rags among the poor.

This struggle of one person's soul caught between a successful military career and poverty wasn't based on the things we normally think about, such as pleasure, security, finding a place in society, and raising a family. The struggle was between worldly success and what pleased God, as taught by the church fathers. In the end, Saint Francis tried to embody those values that pleased God; in fact he directly tried to imitate the life of Jesus and his disciples.

As much as values have changed since the thirteenth century, it's not clear that we are better placed to do the same thing. Money serves to bring pleasure, security, social position, and the ability to raise a family. Those are good values, and there is no reason to suppose that they displease a God who loves his creation. God is not either/or in my view. It isn't that you either live for him or you don't. The process of integrating material life, with all the good is has to offer, and spiritual life, with all the good it has to offer, is a lifelong challenge.

If you live as though money brings the *only* happiness, clearly something has gone wrong. You have neglected the entire world of spirit, with the implication that the surface of life is enough.

Even though we seem to have wandered far from the issue of war and violence, we are actually at the crux, because when people settle for the surface of life they miss the only level that can bring war to an end, which lies beneath the surface.

The word *Maya,* which is usually translated from Sanskrit as "illusion," has many wide-spreading meanings (our modern words *matter, mother,* and *measurement* are related to this root). I prefer to define Maya as "distraction," and without holding moral judgments against money, I must accuse riches of being a terrible distraction. They hold us in the grip of a false self-image, that of being creatures whose purpose on earth is to be prosperous and secure. Our real purpose on earth is very different, as every spiritual tradition recognizes.

We are here to evolve and grow.

We are here to discover who we are.

We are here to transform our surroundings in keeping with who we really are.

Great spiritual teachers have said that we are ultimately here to transcend matter, to worship our maker, to appreciate the infinite creation and learn humility before it. All those things may emerge once we know who we really are. That is life's central mystery, and money doesn't come close to answering it.

The division between matter and spirit faces everyone alike. Though Saint Francis undertook poverty as a noble choice that brought him closer to God, poverty in and of itself isn't noble. He put a particular intention behind his act of renouncing his wealth. The incident, a famous one in Catholic lore, took place when Francesco Bernardo had incensed his father by giving a bag of gold to an impoverished priest so that the priest could rebuild a decrepit church.

The elder Bernardo took his son to court to strip him of his inheritance, and rather than fighting this action, Francesco willingly renounced his fortune, removing his clothes before the judge and handing them to his father. The intention was clear: he wanted to direct his own soul as far from material temptation as possible. That same choice and that same intention are still open to anyone. Yet there are other ways to reach the same end.

Renunciation is not achieved by wearing a hair shirt or a loincloth. Nakedness before God is a symbol for a deeper value, which is closeness to God, a life without separation from one's source. True renunciation is really a shift in allegiance: you shift your attention from the surface of life to the underlying reality. If people were more clear about this, I think a great deal of hypocrisy might come to an end. I mean the hypocrisy of prosperous people who would never sacrifice their money to join with the poor, no matter what Christ or Buddha has to say on the matter. Also the hypocrisy of those who give money to charity and believe that this act in and of itself forgives their spiritual shortcomings.

Rich or poor, we are all caught up in the same system of greed. We have a relationship to money that mirrors our relationship to the material world. The way of peace would change this relationship in many ways. I can see different people doing the following things:

Donating money to peace organizations.

Giving money to the poor.

Refusing to invest in corporations that manufacture arms or are directly involved in military contracts.

Investing in companies that have the least attachment to destructive tendencies, such as harming the environment.

Using one's savings to pay for seasonal retreats and other spiritual work.

This is how money might be well used. But such good actions do not settle the core issue of how you relate to money. The way of peace would be to use your money to further the real reason you are here. Having provided for basic comforts and needs, apply your money to serve the hierarchy of values to which you owe your allegiance. Peace values, as we have seen, are love, evolution, personal growth, discovery, wisdom, harmony, connectedness, and peace itself. If you are using money to further these, you have escaped the grip of one false god: Mammon.

Technology and Well-Being

IN THE 1950S the public first became aware that technology could be deeply immoral and destructive. The turning point came on a rainy July morning in 1945, deep in the New Mexico desert, where a team of scientists and military personnel first successfully detonated an atomic bomb. At the moment that the blast erupted in a blinding flash, the director of the project, Dr. J. Robert Oppenheimer, murmured a quotation from the Bhagavad-Gita, later made legendary: *I am Shiva, the destroyer of worlds.*

If you closely examine the atmosphere inside the shelter where all the project team were gathered, something more mundane was occurring. As one eyewitness reported,

> As the time interval grew smaller and changed from minutes to seconds, the tension increased by leaps and bounds. Everyone in that room knew the awful potentialities of the thing that they thought was about to happen. The scientists felt that their figuring must be right and that the bomb had to go off but there was in everyone's mind a strong measure of doubt. The feeling of many could be expressed by "Lord, I believe; help Thou mine unbelief." We were reaching into the unknown and we did not know what might come of it.

Every event is enmeshed in a tangled hierarchy, and in this case the key words were excitement, awe, suspense, pride, religious doubt, intellect, and will. The sheer excitement of making a great scientific breakthrough was mixed with the certainty that a new epoch was about to dawn, and yet no one knew what it would be like.

That event, if any single event could, set the ethos for our present moment. The unknown did not unfold in a single direction. All the values present in that room in 1945 bore fruit, each in its own way. The enormous excitement over sending the Hubble telescope into space is bound up with the destructive potential of the Star Wars missile shield. The use of lasers can be both deadly and advantageous to life, depending on whether they are used for potential death rays or microsurgery.

Spiritual people generally feel suspicious of technology and therefore reject it. This holds true for a Zen Buddhist aspirant in Connecticut who refuses to watch TV and believes that microwave ovens cause cancer; it also holds true for a devout Muslim in Syria who supports the *fatwah* (a legal opinion or ruling issued by an Islamic scholar) against electricity, in the belief that only the pre-technology world of the Koran is holy. At the same time, we all benefit from technology, and so its spiritual value or lack of it remains troubling.

Even if one picks a weapon that seems diabolical to many observers, it will turn out to be enmeshed with ordinary life. I am thinking now of weapons used and sold by the U.S. that are based on depleted uranium (DU). This material, which is basically the waste product left over from atomic energy plants, happens to be twice as dense as lead (as is true of most radioactive elements that belong to the heavy metal category). Its density makes it perfect for penetrating thick metal armor; therefore DU has become the material of choice for tank-buster warheads and bullets. More than 300 tons of DU were dropped on southern Iraq during and after the first Gulf War in 1991, and it is estimated that the current war brought at least that much more. This fact incites those who oppose the war in Iraq to point to hospital records from

Basra, a city in the heart of the DU area, showing an increase in horrific birth defects. I myself have spoken with a doctor returning from the region who told me of babies born without eyes and fetuses stillborn without heads.

Many symposia have been held on this issue, and two extremes are clear. The U.S. Army, citing its own research and that of independent U.N. teams, points out that there is no residual radiation to be detected in the soil, air, or ground water in places where DU weapons have been used (besides Iraq, Bosnia was another field of war that received heavy DU bombardment). Levels of radioactivity, in fact, are often lower than that which would naturally occur without the presence of DU. The same depleted uranium is used, because of it density, to shield X-ray and MRI machines in hospitals.

On the other side, various experts point to the fact that no one has tested the effect of dust in the air which is left behind after depleted uranium explodes. The bullets and warheads containing DU turn incredibly hot the minute they are fired, and this high temperature not only causes the residual radioactivity to decay very quickly, but it causes the uranium to become a super-fine dust.

Inhaling this dust is unavoidable. It is breathed in by everyone in the surrounding area, friend and foe alike, where DU shells explode. No less a person than the commanding officer who was responsible for decontaminating tanks exposed to DU in the first Gulf War now blames his own severe health problems on DU, calling its use by the U.S. a war crime. In short, one side is claiming that DU is completely harmless and the other side is claiming that it will condemn millions of people to future cancers and birth defects. (DU contamination is already suspected by its opponents of causing the mysterious Gulf War Syndrome that seems to have seriously impacted up to one third of the American soldiers who served in that operation.) Similar weapons are in the arsenals of Britain, France, Russia, and other military powers.

I cannot settle this fiercely emotional debate, but it points out the critical issues with the current state of armaments:

The creativity of humans to invent new weapons is endless.

The effect of advanced weapons on the future is little known.

Weapons developers are not going to give up their research.

The debate is too complex for ordinary citizens to comprehend.

Even if they could comprehend it, citizens have no power in the voting booth to change policies that are deeply embedded in a tight-knit group of powerful bureaucrats and corporations. These groups remain essentially the same no matter which president takes office.

The way of peace asks us to do something difficult, which is to let go of despair. Moral outrage is linked to despair and hopelessness. Perhaps for you the despairing moment came when you saw pictures of Auschwitz being liberated and witnessed the condition of the skeletal inmates and piled corpses. Perhaps for another person the moment came when he saw the photo of the shadow on the sidewalk in Hiroshima that was the only remains of a vaporized human being. Despair is a mask for the belief that the individual no longer matters. The more complex and deadly our technology becomes, the easier it is to say, What can I do? What can anyone do? Things have gone beyond human control. As a peacemaker you will have more power than technology, however, and despair is therefore false.

Military Strength and Security

AT A TIME of record defense budgets and the rise of America as the world's only superpower, military strength is being touted as never before. The subculture that revolves around our bulging military expansion is tight-knit and shares the same values. During the 2004 Republican convention CNN caught two smiling congressmen on their way to a private party for arms dealers and government contractors on a luxurious boat anchored in the Hudson River. These two legislators hold senior positions on the arms committee, which in effect gives them something like carte blanche over decisions that shift billions to one contractor or another. As the outcry over Halliburton contracts has revealed, the same tight-knit club remains in charge year after year. Outsiders may see them as a coterie of death and destruction; they see themselves as privileged managers of the national interest.

The official position of every government worldwide is that military might is totally necessary because it is the only means by which to feel secure in a dangerous world. This shibboleth was trumpeted from the podium at both the 2004 Democratic and Republican national conventions. Let's leave aside the suspicion of opportunism here, since even the most casual observer could tell that the vast majority of delegates on the floor at the Democratic rally were against the war in Iraq, and that their candidate, Senator John Kerry, first made a name for himself by breaking ranks with his military past to oppose the Vietnam War.

Far more crucial is the vulnerability of this particular illusion. Watching New York as the Republicans gathered, one saw a squad of police officers on every block, and thus, we were told, for one week New York was the safest city in the world. How safe was it from:

One person walking down the street with an atomizer spraying the air with a mist of anthrax or smallpox?

One small plane flying over the city's water supply and contaminating it with botulinus?

One band of bombers breaking into a nuclear power plant, such as the one at Indian Point on the Hudson River north of the city?

One brilliant computer hacker disrupting the power grid that serves the entire state?

A superpower, for all its armaments, is as vulnerable to these threats as any nation. The truth is that the safest city in the world is the one where you can walk down the street and need no police officer. The way of peace is our only hope of security. Otherwise, brandishing military might only incites potential terrorists and adds to their number. I am not arguing that armies can be abolished overnight, but that isn't the issue. The issue is that militarism has grown as a world view, and the current threats to every nation can never be ended by the use of massive might.

Like the other false gods, the illusion of military strength is embedded in the tangled hierarchy. The way of peace is the best way to live because it transcends the confusion and fear of the hierarchy represented by the military, the key words for which are:

fear
vigilance
insecurity
belligerence
tough
hard
unyielding
aggressive
masculine

This last word is a reminder that in the name of protecting women, the tangled hierarchy of militarism is starkly male and excludes every desirable feminine value.

At the height of the Cold War, both sides realized that building up their missile force was futile. Once Russia and the U.S. had armed themselves with enough atom bombs to kill the world's population ten times over, the surrealism of their military posturing became obvious. Neither country could launch atomic weapons and hope to survive the counterattack, which meant that their power to bring peace was imaginary.

Military security is even more imaginary today, and yet the old belief in it persists. Our unilateral attack on Iraq that began in 2003 was the first serious exercise of American might since the fall of Soviet Communism fifteen years before. The temptation of unlimited dominance had proved too great for our military strategists. The chance to rule the world was at hand.

Nobody spoke of an actual colonial empire, a model for dominance that was condemned long ago. This was to be a subtler design based on military threat, the implicit understanding around the world that no one could remotely hope to win a victory on the battlefield against the U.S. The new form of dominance also depended on spreading free-market capitalism to every corner of the globe. The final ingredient was democracy, which the U.S. considered the best, if not the only, political system suitable for all countries, if not today then soon.

In this scheme the entire world would be Americanized, and in many regards our empire would be far more total in its grip than Rome or Britain at the height of their conquests. With the arrival of Coca-Cola and MTV, futurists saw an end to superstition, inequality, backward traditions, and oppressive governments everywhere.

But a strange and horrifying thing happened. It turned out that large sectors of the world hated the idea of being Americanized. Estimates of Al-Qaida's strength vary wildly—at most it may contain 200,000 active members. We hear of sleeper cells being situated around the world, waiting for the right moment to spread maximum terror, yet the fact remains that these cells are not the real threat. The real threat is Osama bin Laden's enormous popularity around the globe; a T-shirt with his likeness is said to be the most popular souvenir sold in the Islamic world. He has become a symbol for a mindset that extends far beyond Al-Qaida.

After the ruthless attack on Russian schoolchildren in Beslan in September 2004, the Muslim world was overcome with self-revulsion. Editorials in leading Arabic newspapers recognized that in a few short years a religion of peace has been hijacked by its fanatical element and now has the reputation of being a religion of violence. It is ironic that the Koran arguably exceeds the New Testament in its condemnation of violence and war. A devout Muslim is adjured not to harm any living thing, and even a tree is not to be cut down unless its wood is needed.

Criticism after Beslan was virtually the first time that peaceful, middle-class Arabs have broken ranks, so strong is the bond of tribalism. Yet the Muslim world on the whole still considers bin Laden a hero, in large part because every aspect of the American empire is repugnant to so many Arabs. They don't want to be threatened by American armed might. They don't want their traditional culture overthrown and their belief systems replaced. They don't want American corporations to drive them out of business, and in many cases they don't want to adopt the democratic ways that follow in the wake of free markets. The Muslim ideal envisions a life totally immersed in God, which includes government. This precept is consistent within itself, even though to modern Westerners a return to religious government is repugnant, and even seems, to be totally blunt, barbaric.

Muslims have been roundly condemned for opposing modernism. If they are railing against Americanization, what Muslims offer in reaction seems to be worse: medievalism. The great period of Arab culture flourished during the Middle Ages, and nostalgia for those past glories, fueled by humiliations in recent times as Muslim land was parceled out at the whim of Western powers, has rendered modernism intolerable to many. The tangled hierarchy remains baffling, however, because in another part of their minds most Muslims want all of the advantages of modernism, in terms of prosperity, democracy, and freedom to travel the globe.

I saw an Arab television producer being interviewed at the height of anti-American sentiment during the Iraq war. He was asked where he was going to send his children to college, and without a moment's hesitation, he answered, "M.I.T., or someplace like that." Startled, the interviewer asked why. "Because I want to exchange the Arab nightmare for the American dream," the producer replied. As it happens, he works for Aljazeera, the Arab satellite network that is the most watched news source in the Muslim world. Aljazeera began as a voice of freedom, because its broadcasts, unlike those of official television throughout the Arab dictatorships, are not a pawn of government propaganda. As such, Aljazeera considers itself a force for globalization, even though its managers freely admit that they skew their stories toward Arab interests, just as American networks skew their stories toward American interests. Demonizing Aljazeera, as the administration has consistently done throughout the second Iraq war, shows just how confused people become in the tangled hierarchy. But several things have actually become clear:

The progress of globalization isn't going to halt.

Other cultures will only accept change at their own pace.

Traditional cultures will change at the slowest pace.

Every nation has a right to self-determination, even if America disagrees with the direction it takes.

Americanism is not a replacement for human values.

The gifts of Americanization are not necessarily good just because they benefit America.

The colonial powers of the nineteenth century were certain that their Western Christian values would sweep the world. But one must ask: How can military power force anyone to be Western against their will? How can a war force anyone to accept what someone else thinks is good for him or her? The deeper point isn't that America's atom bombs are useless against terrorists, for that is obvious. The deeper point is that terrorism is equally useless against change. Leaving aside the piteous tragedy of the hostage-taking at the Beslan school, those terrorists were deluded. One child asked them why they had taken over the school, and the answer that came back was, "Our actions here will encourage oppressed Muslims to rise up everywhere." The opposite is true: governments everywhere are rising up against Muslims.

No one can really foresee if American militarism is going to win the war on terrorism, but we know from the way of peace that both sides are engaged in utter futility. The war on terror is just another permutation of violence versus violence. Both sides invoke God. Both sides invoke morality and accuse the other of crimes against humanity. Yet the end result is blindness to reality. By setting your awareness against these illusions, you are bringing change at the level where it has real power, that level where your soul knows the truth and will do everything it can to end blindness and unreality.

DIABOLICAL
CREATIVITY

War has become unbearably brutal. It is deeply disturbing that human nature didn't revolt against our descent into brutality but decided to adapt instead. What makes modern suffering so sinister is that most people have passively accepted living in an atmosphere of fear.

While drinking orange juice in the morning, we gaze blankly at a Madrid railroad station blown apart by terrorists. We listen over dinner to reports of the shock-and-awe campaign that was surgically waged against Baghdad, whose citizens responded with a look of abject terror on their faces (images widely seen around the world but muted on the American TV networks). Iraqis were awed by a liberator who sends burning nuclear waste through their walls, rains tons of shrapnel to tear flesh and organs apart, and blasts homes into rubble with a thirty-foot crater for the ruins to fall into, eliminating any chance of surviving inside. Dismissing these mis-hits as collateral damage doesn't begin to address the terror they engender. Why do we sit still and watch?

The spiritual malaise we have fallen into is well known. It's called alienation, or separation from that which makes a person human. The way of peace brings an end to alienation by restoring the responses that have been lost to numbness. Most people, if they look closely at their lives, know that something has gone seriously wrong. Why do we fixate on empty-headed pop icons and hunger to know every trivial detail of their lives? Why are there no meaningful protests in the streets against the latest weapon of horror? Why do we listen casually while bigots of every stripe rule the radio airwaves? Twenty years ago the number of radio stations that carried shock-jock, or vehemently right-wing talk shows was around a dozen; now the number is over a thousand. One cannot help but think of the truth expressed by W. B. Yeats during the rise of fascism: "The best lack all convictions, while the worst are full of passionate intensity."

Passionate intensity is now rampant. I was startled to read that a class action suit had been filed by some families of victims from the 9/11 attacks against the White House. The suit included President Bush and his top advisors. They were not accused of failing to prevent the terrorist attacks, but of ordering them. At first it was hard to believe what I was reading. The charge being leveled is that the president needed to incite a terrorist event for political gain. The topic of how to manipulate the public through fear had been alive in the minds of certain top advisors for as long as thirty-five years. When the time was right, the suit alleged, the president sent the orders and the hijackers went into action.

Have we really come to this? In the year after the collapse of the twin towers, paranoia reared its head in a vicious rumor that Israel had orchestrated the attacks. Across the Internet spread the allegation that the Jewish workers at the World Trade Center had been warned in advance not to go to work that day. Such is the power of paranoia that the obvious refutation—counting the number of Jews, including Israelis, who died that day—made little impact on those who wanted to believe the story. In Europe, with its more virulent tradition of anti-Semitism, a book that espoused this cruel theory became a bestseller in France. So perhaps it was predictable that the ultimate paranoid fantasy, making our government the agency of attack on its own citizens, would emerge. By the time you read these words, this case will have joined the Internet rumors about the government spreading anthrax, conducting terrorist tests in the New York subway system, and secretly paying off Osama bin Laden.

Falling into such a degraded condition of alienation and mistrust didn't happen all at once. When the poet William Blake looked out at the green English countryside being blackened with smoke belched from factories—a very new development two hundred years ago—he muttered about dark Satanic mills, making an immediate connection between industrialism and hell. He *felt* the despair that was to follow. He refused to be numbed or to quietly accept the inevitable. Blake was a mystic who kept having visions of a paradise that might arise from fallen human nature, but he knew enough to see the huge obstacle that lay before him, nothing less than a change in world view.

> *And did the Countenance Divine*
> *Shine forth upon our clouded hills?*
> *And was Jerusalem builded here*
> *Among these dark Satanic mills?*

His visionary Jerusalem wasn't built and couldn't be, because industrial society was making a definitive choice: Any paradise of the future would have to be scientific. Utopia would be based on inventions. For this anti-spiritual vision to come true, the tangled hierarchy would need to reflect it. Certain values rose to dominate as science marched forward:

efficiency
comfort
progress
rationality
industry
full employment
capitalism
free markets

You and I live by these values today, and yet utopia never happened. What made the first factories satanic in Blake's eyes is still true: if you preserve the old habits of violence and oppression but give them ever more powerful technology to carry out their ends, the result is diabolical. Adaptation to industrial work involved stripping away our humanity one layer at a time. That process is painful, and people resisted. They still resist, as they did in the anarchic demonstration in 1999 when the World Trade Organization met in Seattle. As small but heated bands of protestors threw trash cans through store windows and caused flurries of media-aimed destruction, what most people saw was an irrational tantrum against the benign growth of free trade. The stated purpose of the WTO is for rich countries to help poor countries grow their economies. But in the eyes of the protestors, something much more sinister is at work. As one activist put it, the demonstrations were part of "the growing worldwide backlash against maximizing profits at the expense of the planet."

I am not trying to demonize material progress. Science has

brought some of the comforts it promised, but progress has been corrupting in a very dangerous way. "Things are in the saddle," Ralph Waldo Emerson grimly noted, "and ride mankind." I fully realize that most people do not recognize the insidious dehumanization that has resulted. *I'm not the one doing these bad things* is a common thread in all our thoughts. But to fall short of your spiritual potential is the most basic sign of alienation. You and I are walking around in a state that isn't fully human. To be fully human means being grounded in the infinite creative potential of life. When you are ungrounded, you forget who you are. Outside forces toss you around. You retreat into various distractions that feebly compensate for the immense power and authority you have lost.

I once heard a worried disciple who stood up during a talk by a famous spiritual teacher. "I want to live a spiritual life, but I have to be honest," he said. "I don't want to be poor. I don't want to be uncomfortable and miserable." The audience tittered nervously, thinking about the cold stone on monastery floors and a diet of green tea and rice at four in the morning, but the teacher shrugged. "Why give up anything? Until you achieve unity, your comforts are all you have."

I don't think this was a cynical remark. The potential for suffering that frightened people in the past has been amplified a thousandfold. Knowing that you might die by leaping from a skyscraper to escape burning jet fuel is such a terrifying prospect that it's hard to conceive of anyone who *wouldn't* react with numbness, or with the desire to find a distraction, or with fits of outrage that peter out in passive acceptance.

Can you identify with the stages that one goes through to surrender humanity? The same process engulfs us all. First, a new war, a new weapon, or a new atrocity creates a sense of shock.

One feels repelled and disbelieving. The mind says, *How could this possibly happen?* We get used to the shock and try to block out the fear and shame that underlie our country's participation in it. The authorities inform us that they had no choice. Moral arguments are raised to show why violence was justified. The mind says, *If I want to be safe I'll just have to go along.* We build a layer of numbness around the new level of anxiety that we find ourselves in. The subject of war and death isn't brought up anymore; it feels futile and socially unacceptable. The mind says, *I'm over this now. Everyone else needs to get over it, too.*

When the numbing is complete, we accept the most recent horror as necessary. Technology can't be stopped. It's too bad that evildoers force good people like us into these extreme measures. The mind says, *Everything feels normal again.*

In my lifetime I watched as millions of people followed these steps to get used to the sight of hydrogen bomb explosions, whose fear-inducing effect was so overwhelming that our current weapons, which are subtler but just as ghastly, are greeted with almost no reaction at all. Miniaturized A-bombs packed into a suitcase? Smallpox bacteria mounted in missile warheads? Poison gas released into the subway system? All have been used, or contemplated, yet they create only a minor ripple of horror.

There are moments, however, when individuals discover to their amazement that reality can't be driven away so completely as to hide our essential spiritual nature. I received a message yesterday from a woman who pierced the shield of ordinary life, strangely enough, while giving birth.

She was young and healthy, and up to the moment of delivery her pregnancy was proceeding normally. But as she lay in the hospital having her first contractions, she noticed some alarming symptoms—chest pain, a severe headache, and double vision. Her obstetrician shrugged these off and gave her an Alka-Seltzer. But ten minutes into delivery the woman went into a seizure, which rapidly deteriorated into coma. Unbeknownst to anyone she had suffered two hemorrhages in the brain. Her body went into a condition known as multiple organ failure, from which very few patients recover.

Fearing the worst, her doctor performed a cesarean section and delivered a healthy baby. Still in a coma, the mother was rushed into the ICU, and her family was told that there was realistically no hope. If her liver, kidneys, and other major organs returned, they would never function normally again. The only choices that lay ahead were death or being turned into a chronic invalid under custodial care. The family was advised to hope for the first outcome.

Yet while she was in her coma, the woman wasn't unconscious. What she experienced I'll let her tell in her own words: "When the Buddha was asked about death, he turned over his bowl, meaning a darkness within a darkness. I inhabited that darkness. I became pure consciousness, free of all human ties to family and friends, free of emotion including love and compassion, free of all things but pure awareness. In this way I was in complete peace."

As a spiritual experience, this one is fundamental. Our usual tales about what happens after death, including heavens and hells, journeys into the light and out of it again, don't really touch as truly on the reality of spirit as this woman did. The darkness into which she went is the ground state of existence. Visible reality is built up from this ground state the way a building rises from its foundation. Layer by layer various realities appear. If you are religious, these realities encompass locales like the angelic world or the hundreds of *lokas* in Tibetan Buddhism. If you are a scientist, they encompass the quantum world and the many hidden dimensions of dark matter and energy that black holes open onto.

The spiritual journey takes us to the ground state once again—it is where pure awareness lies, along with unshakable peace. In this woman's case, the proof that she actually went somewhere is undeniable. Not only did she recover from her coma, but five years later her health shows no symptoms from her period of multiple organ failure. She woke up with a totally different awareness of who she is and the purpose of her life:

"I know that God returned me to earth and to good health for a reason," she said. "I have yet to fulfill my destiny, which includes raising my son and writing and lecturing about spirituality." Her personal commitment is all the stronger because, as it happens, this woman is a Muslim, now living in San Francisco.

As we walk the streets engaged in daily life, you and I aren't aware of the ground state of reality. But it is aware of us. Just as a building would collapse without a foundation, the world of the five senses depends upon the invisible support of infinite intelligence. It depends upon consciousness. It depends upon natural laws that permeate every atom. You and I embody those things, and although we might not experience the degree of pure awareness I've just described, if we regain even a bit of it we can escape suffering. The steps aren't complicated. In fact there is only one: Going deeper every day into the potential for change that underlies your life.

Let me give you a description of your life not as you see it but as ripples of awareness that move outward from a center.

Center: Pure awareness, pure being, pure peace.

First Wave: Consciousness stirs. There is still no time or space. The only quality to emerge is a faint vibration.

Second Wave: The faint vibration realizes that it is conscious. At the same moment it realizes that it can create anything. Life has appeared, and starts to move quickly.

Third Wave: Creation dawns, with invisible properties that will turn into material things and subjective experiences. These properties include intelligence, bliss, organization, unfoldment through time, expansion into space. Up to now everything has been unified. Now that unity has split apart.

Fourth Wave: Creation bursts forth into a million fragments, each changing at every second into a million more. But consciousness isn't worried about losing control, because the balance still favors unity. The creator is firmly inside creation.

Fifth Wave: The outer world follows its own laws. Consciousness is apparently not in control, acting as a spectator only. It can sit back and enjoy the play of *Lila,* the dance of creation. At this stage mind appears, meaning the ability to reflect upon what is happening.

Sixth Wave: Mind begins to feel separate. A single observer becomes countless observers, each with its own life journey, each with its own viewpoint. At this stage ego is born.

Seventh Wave: The creation is now endlessly fascinating. Outer events dominate. The creator is lost in his creation. There seems to be nothing the individual can do to stop the machinery.

Here on the outer wave, suffering is a fact of life. This must be so, because separation is a fact of life, and the two go hand in hand. Fortunately, reality is dynamic. There was never a single creation. Wave after wave of creativity is moving out from the ground state at every second. Depending on your awareness, you can catch any wave. Then everything that seems fixed and immovable changes, and the change isn't by bits and pieces; it's a unity that affects everything.

The next wave of evolution will bring a world we wouldn't recognize from where we are now. For one thing, the hints we have that consciousness is everywhere will become a certainty. As I write these words in the autumn of 2004, the third of three violent hurricanes has struck with devastating impact. The first, hurricane Charley, was more than a typical seasonal nuisance. It cut a swath of destruction across the center of Florida that called for major emergency relief. On its heels came hurricane Frances. Frances was as big as Texas and lingered for thirty hours over the state of Florida; only by chance did its Force 5 winds decrease before it landed. Within days hurricane Ivan, also remarkably huge, drifted up from the Caribbean, landing on the Gulf Coast with 130 mile-per-hour winds and a series of deadly tornadoes in its wake. Ordinary people have begun to ask strange questions:

Is this string of storms an accident or is something else going on?

Has nature turned against us?

Did this happen to Florida because of the infamous political doings in that state during the 2000 elections?

Is God saying, Don't do it again?

The underlying question comes down to this: Are we causing earth changes? The spiritual answer is, of course we are, because Mother Nature is disturbed by our lack of love and respect for her. The scientific answer is, of course we are, but only indirectly through decades of reckless pollution. Everything depends on what level of consciousness dominates your awareness. All answers are tangled, yet in the untangling I believe that science will one day connect earth changes and human awareness. Natural disasters are not a message from God but a message from ourselves.

The great spiritual traditions have clearly mapped how a person regains the status of a creator. As power returns, everything changes in ways that cannot be guessed at in the state of alienation and separation.

A ROAD MAP TO CREATION

How things get better as consciousness evolves

You begin to feel again; numbness lifts.
You regain a sense of being benign. You belong here and are
  cherished.
Your desires turn from self-destructive to self-empowering.
Your thoughts have a benign effect on your environment.
Reality shifts in an evolutionary direction for everyone else.
The laws of creation reemerge under the control of human
  awareness.
It becomes commonplace to live from the level of the soul.

All these changes occur by degree, steadily growing stronger
as a person goes deeper inside. Spiritual evolution doesn't exist
just to make you feel better. It exists to restore you to power and
authenticity. The slogan "You create your own reality" has become a cliché, but it never stops being true. A creator who feels
powerless is still in charge of reality, but there is such confusion
inside that the whole process is cloaked. When people ask, Why
don't my dreams come true? the answer is that they are coming
true, but when you have dreams that conflict with each other, that
mix fantasy and true vision, that are laced with fear and anger, it's
no wonder that the results are confusing. You and I were put here
as creators, but what good does that do us if we shrink in terror
from our own diabolical creations?

To be spiritual doesn't mean turning your back on technology. In the 1970s when the Khmer Rouge guerrillas overran
Cambodia and installed Pol Pot as dictator, a million people died
in a vast rebellion against progress. Every person known to have a

college education was executed. Automobiles and other machines associated with the decadent West were smashed. Urban populations were shipped out to the countryside, and in a few years oxcarts used paved highways to crush rice and remove the chaff—this in the absence of the farm machines that had been destroyed. Returning to the past became its own version of hell.

The choice isn't between the past and the future. Science is not going to lose its dominance any time soon. To live in peace with that fact, you and I must restore a self-image that is spiritual and human in its essence. A saint doesn't become less holy by driving a car, but a human being becomes less human by supporting states that build mega-weapons.

Science is going to keep finding new ways to build killing machines until we transform our image of who we are. Here are some of the accepted principles, all part of our current world view, that block spiritual evolution.

THE HUMAN ANIMAL

How science distorts human nature

We are basically animals, an evolved mammal.

Our behavior is governed by our animal nature, which has remained intact over millions of years.

Animal nature is imprinted in our genes and therefore in our brain.

We do whatever the chemical reactions in our brain dictate.

A certain portion of the brain is rational, and this higher brain produces the best in human behavior.

The world has become a better place because of the dominance of reason over irrational impulses.

These are fundamental principles you and I have learned to adapt to. They are the same principles we must stop adapting to if we want to end war and violence, because under the guise of being rational and objective, this line of reasoning has created the hellish machinery of war.

We are basically animals, an evolved mammal.

The moment you see yourself as an animal, it becomes easier to kill someone else. The old world view that gave human beings a soul contained a moral imperative that doesn't hold true anymore. *Thou shalt not kill* isn't a law animals obey. After Darwin, religious people either conceded the truth of evolution or attempted to fight a rear-guard action in defense of the prescientific belief that God created the world as it is, without evolution. But that struggle is really a social one; the heart of the matter lies elsewhere, in the Darwinian tenet that all animals evolved by a life-or-death struggle, which means that our species did the same. We succeeded by becoming good killers.

I don't think anyone has to shrink from the physical evidence of evolution. Our ancestors may have succeeded through violence—there is plenty of evidence to say that they succeeded through community as well—but we have evolved immensely since then. Our human forebears existed for at least 500,000 years without fire, but once the Stone Age arrived we evolved into creatures who use fire and take it for granted. The whole discussion around being animals has little bearing on the major progress that early humans made, not only the taming of fire but the advent of the wheel, weaving, farm cultivation, and houses. These are all nonviolent steps of evolution, and each one took place independent of our animal nature. Undomesticated animals are fated to live outside, hunt for food, and die of random accidents and disease, but we aren't. Evolving to be at peace won't change the past; it will make it irrelevant.

Our behavior is governed by our animal nature, which remains intact.

If the first point isn't true, this one can't be either. The equation between human and animal nature is crude and usually moralistic. Gangs roaming the streets to commit crimes get labeled "animals"; so do husbands who leave their wives for younger, more attractive women. Wars are described as extensions of meat-eating predators attacking peaceful grazing animals, or a new species killing off an old one through ruthless competition. These comparisons only serve to make us feel ashamed. They are degrading both to us *and* to animals. I can observe the animal nature in myself without being ashamed of it. I eat, breathe, excrete, have sex, and inhabit a physical body because these are my animal inheritance. There is no conflict with spirit in any of these things. The old religious prejudice against the body in favor of the soul blinds us to a simple fact: There is no shame in being a mammal, given the beauty and wonder of the animal world.

If violence is called an animal trait, it has to be countered that animals don't kill for sport, exterminate populations of other animals out of thoughtless greed, or use violence to feel important or defeat goodness. Those are all human developments, and only after we take responsibility for them do we have the right to blame our animal past. Blaming the past is pointless anyway, since violent acts are instigated by decisions in the present.

Animal nature is imprinted in our genes and therefore in our brain.

Every behavior has a genetic imprint. There is no reason to focus on only our so-called lower nature. Altruism is imprinted in our genes; many creatures beneath us on the evolutionary ladder will sacrifice their lives to save their offspring or defend a colony at the risk of dying themselves. A honeybee dies after it uses its stinger, yet the hive survives.

Genes don't distinguish between high and low behavior. Love and nurturing are genetically imprinted behaviors; so is language going back tens of millions of years. (We've been hearing for decades about porpoise language, but an Australian sheep dog in Germany was trained by researchers to comprehend 200 human words, as many as a chimpanzee.) The most sophisticated functions among humans, such as my ability to type out these words, is rooted in brain structure. It will probably turn out that spirituality is too. Everything spiritual is experienced as thoughts, feelings, or actions, all of which depend on DNA. So if you want to blame genes for violence, you have to blame them for sainthood, too.

We do whatever the chemical reactions in our brain dictate.

When you think you are being yourself, are you really just the end-product of chemicals? This is a form of determinism that many people assume must be true. When medicine can relieve depression by altering levels of serotonin in the brain; when anxiety, obsessive compulsions, attention deficits, and schizophrenia can be relieved in the same way, the evidence mounts that *all* behavior is rooted in brain chemistry.

Neurology does locate various behaviors in specific portions of the brain, with the implication that these are control centers, switches that go on and off to make us feel what we feel and do what we do. The fallacy here is that the same sections of the brain light up when we want them to or when someone else does. If a patient suffering from OCD, or obsessive-compulsive disorder, is viewed through an MRI machine, specific areas of the brain show up as abnormal. If a drug such as Prozac is given, these areas return to more normal functioning. But if the patient goes into couch therapy, using no drugs at all, the obsessive behavior will often improve, and the related areas of the brain will return to normal functioning. What this means is that brain chemistry isn't the primary cause of change, only the indicator.

We already know that women with breast cancer can increase their chance of survival by joining therapy groups and talking about their condition. Empathy and a sense of connectedness change the brain, and it in turn sends signals that change the body. If healing works, it's because we can make choices that override brain function. Certainly we depend on having healthy brains in order to participate in life. You can't listen to music if your radio is broken, but that is far from saying that radios compose music. A healthy brain exists to carry out your instructions— you are the composer, it is your instrument.

A certain portion of the brain is rational, and this higher brain produces the best in human behavior.

Nobody questions that the cerebral cortex is the center for higher thought and reasoning. But it is grossly misleading to call the higher brain the sole source of progress, as if it has to defeat the lower brain in a constant, never-ending war. The lower brain is instinctive; our emotions are centered there. Certain senses, such as smell, are directly wired to the lower brain. But none of this is to say that the higher brain and its capacity for reason gave us civilization.

For one thing, reason gave us horrific weapons and made war diabolical. It did this precisely by disconnecting from emotions and instincts. Our great enemy isn't irrationality, it's imbalance. The human brain is orchestrated naturally as a whole. Through brain imaging we now can see with our own eyes that every thought is like a symphony, with various sections of the brain lighting up at once, each in concert with the other. There was never a neurological turf war going on inside us. You can't think of a single word like peace or a single image, like seeing the world at peace, without using your whole brain.

The lower brain is the chief agent of bonding. When you look into someone's eyes and recognize a loving expression, what's actually happening is irrational, in the pure sense that your brain is bypassing the cortex and going directly to its intuitive and emotional centers. Those centers let you know if you can trust someone. Bypassing rational analysis, we know instantly whether another person is in tune with us. These intuitive signals are always coming in, but the higher brain can choose to ignore them. They get shut out of the symphony and aren't heard. This exclusion lies at the root of alienation. An alienated person has one dominant feeling: disconnection.

In the disconnected state the higher brain cannot substitute for lost functions. Morality can't fight the emotions of fear, isolation, loneliness, and a vague sense of always being unsafe. Those feelings roam the mind unless the lower brain receives reassurance from the higher brain. We aren't nurturing that reassurance. Instead we have excluded it. By closing off the channels of feeling and intuition, we allow the higher brain freedom to pursue the diabolical side of science. A friend of mind was contemplating one of the vociferous warmongering hawks on television and said, "So many of them are like rocks." The lower brain doesn't deserve to be labeled as the root of savagery. It contains the softness of love and feeling, the sense of being at one with other creatures, that can melt even rocks.

The world has become a better place
because of the dominance
of reason over irrational impulses.

I recently saw a video of a troubled child whose behavior was so extreme that his mother said, "I can hardly bring myself to use these words, but I am afraid of my own child. His eyes sometimes look like a demon's." The child, a nine-year-old boy, had developed full-blown symptoms of a psychopath. He started fires in secret. He tortured small animals, had a fascination with knives, and threw tantrums in which he would beat his head against the wall. On occasion he threw feces or smeared it on the wall. He could be sweet and gentle, yet without notice these moods would turn into rage.

The parents tried to be understanding. They took their son to doctors, taking stabs at one therapy after another. No sort of drug treatment seemed to help. But a canny psychiatrist noticed that the whole family dynamic was warped. The parents were trying hard to love their child, but this was mostly the higher brain saying, You must, you should, it's the right thing to do. Emotionally they kept a huge distance from their boy, finding themselves unable to really love or praise him, to look at him with unfeigned affection, to tolerate and forgive him. Starting from a base of inattention, they drew farther and father back, in response to which their child became more and more destructive. This child's behavior seems like a metaphor for the outcast lower brain. Science has condemned the lower brain as it exalted reason to the detriment of humanity. We have made unreason a demon, and now it acts like one.

Outside the precinct of the higher brain is a magical domain, as many people have discovered when they walk away from the failed utopia of science. Irrationality doesn't rule there in place of reason. An expanded mind is still rational, but it includes much more. All the tools a creator needs are at hand, and the labels of reason and unreason are irrelevant. What's relevant is increasing your skill at creation. The way of peace, as you realize by now, I'm sure, depends upon acquiring the confidence to say, This is my world, and it runs as my vision of perfection wants it to run.

This may sound more arrogant than any claim of science, but I think the underlying truth is humble. When we abandon our claim to be conquerors of nature, the universe freely gives us the gifts we were trying to gain by force. The deepest mystery of all is that each person is more powerful than the seemingly iron laws that control us. A woman I trust told me the following story. All her life she had been someone who was attracted to psychics and healers. Her background in a suburb of Fort Worth didn't support her fascination, but somehow the seed was planted. At twenty-two she was a grade school teacher living in a small house with a husband who sold cars. At forty-two she was divorced, earned her living as a mind-body therapist, and completely surrendered to whatever spirit wanted her to do.

For a time she was led to explore the practice of Huna, the healing system that Hawaiian kahunas follow. This system is known for massages and other forms of body work, but she went deep into its esoteric aspects. One thing the kahuna kept repeating is that our bodies are just mental projections, and that we can heal them instantly using the mind. "That seemed true to me," she said, "and one day when I was slicing vegetables, I looked down and noticed that I had gashed my hand. A red line of blood was already starting to ooze out. Instantly I had the thought, I can heal this. I don't remember doing anything else, but when I looked down, the gash was gone. There was no evidence that I had cut myself. I stopped and pulled the skin to see if I could find where I'd cut myself, but not even the faintest line was visible.

"You know, since then I've had all sorts of cuts and bruises. I never heal them, or even think to. Sometimes I do stop and say to myself, This is stupid. You understand what's possible. Why don't you just make this cut go away? I wish I had an answer."

The answer is that at first we only glimpse deeper reality in random flashes. It was the instantaneous impulse to heal that made her erase the first wound. There was no hesitation or doubt. The wound and the healer met in a precise fit. Which is to say that healing is a place inside one's awareness, and if you have access to that place, the normal rules governing the body no longer apply. On subsequent occasions, this woman couldn't mesh her mind and the moment.

Peace involves all the things this story teaches. Peace will be achieved when we mesh our minds with an outbreak of violence and say, with total confidence, I can heal that. Like healing a gash in the hand, peace comes from a place we need to access. It isn't a future event we need to wait for. Peace is a reality that exists on a wave of consciousness that is closer to the center than we are now. I don't mean to make this sound esoteric or mystical. But we have to become aware of the laws of consciousness before reality will ever shift permanently. For the moment there will be more and more glimpses of peace, I'm sure. With each one we will learn to master more of the laws of consciousness, and eventually they will be mastered. These include:

the law that physical reality is a product of consciousness

the law that power is greater as one gets closer to the ground state of being

the law that mass events are images in collective consciousness the law that physical reality offers up miracles only when consciousness allows them to emerge

The way of peace is a new laboratory in which these laws are explored. You can explore them to whatever depth you wish. You don't have to wait on science; there is no need for technicians and specialists. This is the laboratory of spirit, and the hypothesis you are trying to prove is your own soul.

THE POLITICS
OF THE SOUL

YOU ACTUALLY THINK your vote's going to make a difference? I'm surprised at you, Deepak. I thought you knew
better."

My old friend Andrew showed up late for our rendezvous.
He used to be Andy when I first met him back in the 1970s. The
last year he cast a vote for president was 1972. I remember it took
a long time before he scraped off his bumper sticker that read
DON'T BLAME ME, I'M FROM MASSACHUSETTS.

He laughs when I mention it. "You're dating yourself," he
says. That was the bumper sticker that announced you had voted
for George McGovern in the 1972 election, the year Richard
Nixon carried every state but Massachusetts.

Other things changed for Andrew around then. Because of
Vietnam, the draft, Watergate, and the tenor of the times, he gave
up on politics and began to move in a spiritual direction. The
next bumper sticker said RECOVERING CATHOLIC, followed by
the current one, PRACTICE RANDOM ACTS OF KINDNESS.

"I just saw a disgusting statistic on CNN," he says. "Did you
know that eighty-six percent of people who go to church once a

week or more intend to vote for Bush?" He takes an angry chomp from his veggie BLT sandwich. "I mean, that's *any* church, not just the fundies."

"So at least you're still emotional about the election," I say.

"I'm a bundle of emotions. Attachment is one of my big issues."

And so we jumped into the question of whether spiritual people should vote. Does any vote really make a difference? Aren't you already doing enough for the world without giving in to this pointless ritual? Does voting make you a good citizen but a bad saint? Andrew draws a sharp distinction between spirituality and religion. He doesn't see himself as a believing Catholic anymore, therefore the dictum of "Render unto Caesar what is Caesar's" is no longer part of his vocabulary. He rises at dawn for his long daily meditation, eats his organic vegetables, takes his massages, and reads—quite seriously, though I am poking some fun at him—in the scriptures of every faith.

All of which makes him disappointed that I would still be trudging into the polling booth after all these years.

Here's the gist of what I told him: to be spiritual is to realize many things, and one is that everyone is connected. When you act, you affect every moment of your life. You also affect every moment in everyone else's life. Because we are all connected, you can't turn your back on that fact. Being connected creates a new kind of power for the individual.

It may seem that a simple social act like casting a ballot is a tiny gesture. In an atmosphere of intolerance it can seem like a fruitless gesture as well.

But it isn't. A single vote contains a mystery. The mystery is wrapped up in the concept of the soul and what it means to have one.

I realized from the first day of writing this book that every issue in it was a hot issue, and practically every chapter could begin with a newspaper article on war, terrorism, nationalism, and so on. What I didn't expect was to read a discussion of the soul in an article in the *New York Times* entitled "The Duel Between Body and Soul." I began reading with eager interest, because the author, a Yale psychology professor named Paul Bloom, was arguing against the notion that bodies and souls are two different things.

In the context of the heated social wrangle over abortion, many people, using commonsense dualism, want scientists to tell them exactly when a cluster of fertilized cells in a mother's womb becomes human, as if there might be a precise moment when the soul enters the body, or to put it in modern terms, when the mind becomes consciously human.

Professor Bloom points out that science will never deliver such an answer, because child development and the history of evolution both show that consciousness arrives through a very gradual process. It shows up in almost invisible changes, therefore a biologist cannot spot the first creature on earth that was conscious, nor point to the moment that a fetus becomes mindful.

At this point in the article my heart sank, because Bloom went on to say that the soul is an illusion. When the brain lights up in a certain region, *that* is the mind, and nothing more, which is to say that you are the end-product of brain chemistry.

As a defender of the soul, I must show a way for it to be something more than brain chemistry. There is a fine line to draw here, because the religious notion of the soul has become so degraded that it is no longer useful. I wish this weren't so. Sadly, I find that the most closed minds exist among religious people, not because they are rigid or fanatical (those types don't want to even begin a discussion), but because religious people have a preset notion of concepts like God and soul. Their minds seek evidence that validates what they already know to be true. This attitude is as binding as the scientific attitude. One is based on faith in unseen things, the other in total skepticism about unseen things.

Why is this pertinent to a book on how to end war and violence? Because the central subject is consciousness. War erupts from people's consciousness, from a level deeper than ordinary life. An attack like 9/11 incites a visceral, reflexive reaction that spreads throughout society, leaving almost no room for disagreement. Even those people who now strongly oppose the second war in Iraq moved gradually toward that position. They were entrenched in the anger and blame that swept our society.

The soul lies deeper than anger and blame. If it is to have any effect in bringing about peace, the soul has to become just as accessible as anger and blame. This isn't easy right now. After 9/11 people did not feel waves of compassion once their anger wore off; nor were there many who skipped the stage of anger and blame. The way of peace says that no action is more powerful than action from the soul. Yet this is a theoretical statement until we know what the soul is and how to reach it. Only then can an apparently simple act like casting a ballot turn out to have real power.

Here are the standard attributes of the soul as seen by religions.

WHAT IS THE SOUL?

The religious viewpoint

The soul is a spark of the divine.
It exists before birth and will survive after death.
It lives with God.
God has placed a soul inside each person.

Souls are pure and untouched by earthly affairs.
We feel our souls as a source of higher emotions and uplift.
The soul is holy in a way that the flesh can never be.

A scientist might dismiss this view automatically, because not a single point can be validated using objective measures. And if the soul is totally subjective, or if it exists in the mystical realm of the divine, it lies outside scientific interest. Of course, the fact that science can't see a thing doesn't make it unreal. No one has ever seen a neutrino, but that doesn't prevent belief in its existence. As with all forms of prejudice, the scientific prejudice tends to be rigid in what it accepts and rejects.

WHAT THE SOUL ISN'T

The scientific rejection of higher consciousness

The mind can be explained without dragging in references to
  God.
Nobody knows what precedes birth or follows after death. All
  we can study is the mind here and now.
The mind is located in the brain, not with God.
There is no evidence of anything inside the brain except a
  complex of chemical and electrical activity.
If you change the brain, the mind changes at the same time.
  There is no part of us that is untouchable and unworldly.
Higher emotions are nothing but the predominance of
  certain neurotransmitters like serotonin and dopamine.
The body, being the center of all chemical activity, *creates* the
  mind. There is nothing else the soul could be, except a
  physical phenomenon.

The underlying disagreement here is profound. In simplest terms, the religious person believes that God is behind all material creation, while the scientist asserts that material creation can run itself, thank you very much, without any need for an outside hand. As with most dichotomies, people who eavesdrop on this argument feel pressure to choose one side or the other, hence the divisiveness over the hot issues of abortion and stem cell research. Lines have been drawn, not on the basis of fact, but on the basis of worldview. If you already know that the soul is divine, you'd never risk defiling it in the cold harshness of a laboratory (never mind that the same divine spark is being extinguished every day on the battlefield). If you know that there is no reality outside material reality, you'd never begin to take seriously the notion that there are unholy acts (never mind that science hasn't come close to explaining where consciousness actually came from).

The way of peace says that you will never access the power of the soul if you buy into this dichotomy. The soul is a living, dynamic part of each person. It exists as consciousness and therefore must be found in consciousness. Everything the brain experiences is a manifestation of the soul. The soul permeates our cells, but it isn't inside anything, just as it isn't outside anything. If you want to experience your soul, which is absolutely possible, you must go beyond the more superficial levels of emotion and personality. This journey is a journey of knowledge and power. As you embark on it, everyday actions no longer mask the soul; they express its dynamic creative energy. In other words, touching the soul alters reality.

The way of peace is a soul journey to acquire the ability to change reality. How can you convince anyone of this fact who has not taken the first step? I sometimes imagine a great violinist who has become stranded in a country that has never heard music. His violin has been lost with the rest of his luggage, and he finds himself being asked by the children of this country, "What is music? We've never heard of such a thing."

"Well," he says, "it's the most beautiful experience in the world."

"Is it a sound?" the children ask. "Is it like the wind or a bear growling?"

"Yes," he says hesitantly, "but the sound of music is more like birdsong."

So the children start twittering like birds. One of them proposes shooting some birds so that music can be extracted from their bodies. Perhaps it can be cooked up into music soup that they can all eat.

The violinist is alarmed. "Music isn't in the birds. Music is an art; it comes from beauty itself."

The children are baffled. "Show us your music," they say. But the violinist has no instrument, and unfortunately he has landed in a place where God prohibits singing (as he once did in medieval Europe). He despairs that anyone will ever know what music really is.

The soul has its own music that can only be hinted at through words. I am not speaking of religious epiphanies, though they are very real. In most people's lives the growth of consciousness doesn't move by epiphany. Someone might have a breakthrough or a turning point that feels as if he or she were directly touched by spirit. But for the most part consciousness grows and deepens by degrees. The soul isn't a thing. It is much closer to art, which grows and deepens the more you devote yourself to it.

What science can't explain, it doesn't see. This includes beauty, devotion, faith, inspiration, nobility, compassion, empathy, fate, intuition, and love itself. Are we really claiming these are fictions or illusions? In fact, they make life worth living.

I venture to argue that the view I've just outlined—that the soul is the origin of consciousness—appears in every spiritual tradition. The fact that it is distorted in popular religion and dismissed by science is a matter of politics, not a matter of proof. Religious thinkers are forced to pretend that their area of ignorance is trivial, and so must the scientific side. Yet the areas of ignorance are quite large on both sides. Religious people refuse to look deeply into consciousness for fear that somebody will convince them that all their faith in unseen things is superstition, or worse. The scientific side refuses to admit their ignorance about the existence of a non-material reality for fear that they will be led into irrational, wooly thinking.

The way of peace aims for the very heart of reality. No one is entitled to a fixed opinion about the outcome, because each journey is unique. The musician finds the essence of beauty, the scientist the essence of reason. The devoted mother finds the essence of motherhood, the wounded child finds the essence of compassion. Everything is shaped to who you are. Yet the journey is also universal. Having been traversed thousands of times over the centuries, the path to the soul has revealed certain fundamentals.

TRUE FOR YOU, TRUE FOR EVERYONE

The fundamentals of consciousness

Awareness has depth.
The deeper you go, the more reality will change.
Reality is dependent upon your state of consciousness.
As your awareness goes deeper, it acquires more power.
This power can change the world, both inside and out.
There are no facts that cannot be influenced by awareness.
Ultimately your awareness creates everything you experience.

Reading this list, I can imagine someone saying, Well, if all this is true for everyone, then it must be true for religious people *and* scientists. Happily, it is. People from every walk of life have stepped into the invisible realm. The scientific label for this place is quantum, although it would be more fair to call it quantum with a difference. The difference is that humans—and not just quarks and superstrings—have a place in the invisible realm.

The strange behavior of the subatomic world has been known for a hundred years, since the great breakthrough of Einstein and his generation, who proved that physical reality isn't remotely what it seems. By now the public is well aware that time isn't really a straight line, that matter isn't really solid, that observers change what they observe, and that uncertainty rules any seemingly fixed event.

Physicists are stubborn about reserving this realm for subatomic particles, but I see no reason why the cautions of science must be regarded as law. Physicists may know quarks, but human beings have experienced a vastly wider world for a long time, and from that world we get intimations of the soul. Having experienced these intimations, we ask for them to be explained. I'd like to illustrate this with the story of Julian, a man in his fifties who recounted his life as we sat together one day in the home of a mutual friend.

Julian comes from rural Texas and had a traditional Baptist upbringing. He doesn't describe himself as an extraordinary child, but I imagine, considering what came next, that he might not have been all that ordinary. When he was in his mid-thirties Julian's father was seriously injured in a car accident by a drunk driver.

"The next time I saw him was in the ICU," Julian recounts. "He was hooked up to machines and unconscious. The doctors shook their heads, making no predictions, but preparing us for the possibility that my father's coma might be permanent. I visited him every day, and on one of these visits, when the two of us were alone in his room, a strange idea struck me. Actually, it was more than an idea.

"I knew that if I touched him, my father would regain consciousness and fully recover. I don't know where this realization came from. I wasn't a healer, I had never been interested in healing. Maybe because of that, I had the notion that I would be exchanging my life for his. I literally thought at that moment I would die in order for him to live.

"Despite this, I didn't hesitate. I laid my hands on my father's chest, and at that instant he sat up. He looked at me, and the first words out of his mouth were 'I love you, son.'

"That was the decisive event that changed my life. I have never healed anyone since, and I didn't tell a soul, including my father, what had happened. But I took a different path from that moment on."

Julian began to pay attention to dreams and coincidences. He looked for clues about what he should do with his life. One night he had a dream in which he saw himself holding the hands of children, with snow-capped peaks in the distance. The next day the opportunity to go to Tibet arrived out of the blue; on his trip Julian founded a private orphanage. Another time a vision led him to do humanitarian work in India. The guiding principle of his life became to pay attention to messages that came from some place deeper than the superficial layer of personality and ego drives.

I know nothing more about this man, but it seems to me that he is living the way of peace. Not that peace always leads to humanitarian work or altruistic devotion, but if you pay attention to the impulses of the soul, you will be drawn deeper and deeper into the heart of reality. You will approach the workshop where reality is made, and as you come closer you will witness that the only maker of reality is yourself.

I began with my friend Andrew, who opted out of politics and most other worldly affairs, in order to be more spiritual. I hope he reads these pages, because what he is seeking is not found only in seclusion. Consciousness reaches into every aspect of life. All our divisions between inner and outer exist so that we can make sense of two worlds which seem to be separate. Eventually they merge, and as that occurs, a person ceases to be a cause for private change and turns into a cause for universal change.

What do people carry in with them when they close the curtain of the voting booth? They carry their political convictions, whether they align with the right or the left. They carry their sense of civic duty. They carry their emotions. But deeper down, aren't they also carrying their whole lives? If living in the moment means anything, it means that each moment of existence is a point that contains everything. In a mysterious way, to act is to express the universe, and like the still point of the revolving world, each act is both in time and outside it.

Spiritual people aspire to be in both places, timebound and timeless. In India this is sometimes expressed as "the lamp at the door"—your soul is poised, as if on a threshold between the everyday events that occur in time and the background of the unchanging, infinite absolute. The reason this is important is that if you can live from the level of your soul, you are doing something very special. It doesn't really matter what actions you take. The important thing is how much consciousness you add to the whole of human existence, for that is how eternity expresses itself, like a lamp shining in through the window of eternity.

A great soul like Buddha or Jesus wasn't just a lamp at the door; they were beacons. You and I may feel smaller than Buddha or Jesus, yet that is an opinion formed by our egos. Spiritually, all the light being expressed through a human being is equal, at least in terms of quality. Why? Because light is a metaphor for the power of consciousness. Everyone's consciousness draws from the same underlying reality. But it doesn't really matter if history will remember you as a great soul. At this moment you are expressing the entire universe through your consciousness. The cosmic plan, whether we call it divine or not, doesn't need you or me to reach its ultimate fulfillment. Yet the parts you and I play are unique. No one can duplicate them; we make our own cosmic history every second.

SO WHAT IS the world becoming and what are we becoming? I'd like to think that we are becoming a new humanity, but I may be wrong. My vote won't hasten that new humanity, nor will it retard it. What my vote will do is put consciousness into action. I'm not saying that's a virtue. I am not hoisting myself above those well-intentioned spiritual people who pursue their private disciplines and choose to ignore most of Caesar's realm.

I am connected to everything in the world. This is the realization that takes me to the polls. I step into the booth not as a dutiful citizen, a political animal, or a bundle of emotions even though I am all of those things. I am essentially one strand in the web of consciousness, and when my little strand trembles, the universe notices. Voting is an act of consciousness, and as such I think the votes of spiritual people are actually more powerful than the votes of unconscious people. Your hand on the voting lever is affecting the world as surely as the lifting of Buddha's hand in a mudra of peace or the teaching of Jesus that announced love as a force in the cosmos.

(STILL) MAD AS HELL

I DON'T KNOW how long you've been in Atlanta, but you sure don't know much about the South."

The man at the lecture was right. He was a stranger with a heavy drawl who had come out of the audience one night in Atlanta. I had dropped a remark he took exception to when I said that long-held beliefs can change. My example was the deep South, where people no longer defend the practice of slavery and the civil war that resulted from it.

"We haven't forgotten, we just know how to behave better," the man said. I looked at him, gauging behind his smile whether he meant what he was saying. Had I stepped into a minefield whose charges were laid a hundred and fifty years ago? I knew enough to recognize that the South is reputed to be the most bellicose part of America, the part that backs every war and sends the highest proportion of its young to fight, the part that gets infuriated at the very mention of a peace movement.

"So peace is a fighting word in the South?" I asked.

"Almost," the man said, his smile fading from friendly to ironic. "You'd have to live here to understand."

The issue of long-held grievances is crucial to most wars. The cause of today's conflict is buried in yesterdays hostilities, which should have died out long ago. Only they haven't. Memory keeps old causes alive, and as it was with the Civil War, the embittered side is always the one that lost. I was told that in Atlanta nobody has forgotten that in 1864 General William Tecumseh Sherman, under orders from Abraham Lincoln to bring the South to its knees, burned the city to the ground in his infamous march to the sea. Yet there are no survivors of that event, and no children of survivors. Who exactly is doing the remembering here? Grandchildren of ghosts?

Memory keeps anger inflamed in families, countries, and the world; therefore we have to look at how this mechanism works if the way of peace is going to prevail. Consider your own past and find an incident that still arouses anger in you, something that makes you say to yourself, I should be over this. I should rise above it and let it go. But I'm still mad as hell. For most people it's not hard to find such an incident. Perhaps you have survived a bitter divorce or custody battle. When you think back to it, what memories arise? How are they connected and tangled up with each other?

Something of the following elements are at work.

THE CHEMISTRY OF ANGER

Why the past continues to haunt

I can't get over what was done to me.
It wasn't fair.
Love and trust became empty words.
I acted on my worst impulses, but so did the other side.
Events took on a life of their own.

I was blind.

I made stupid decisions because I was so angry and hurt.

No one cared enough about my hurt.

They wanted to humiliate me.

I was afraid I might lose control.

The first thing this list tells us is that anger isn't simple. Humiliation enters into it (ask anyone from a country that has lost a war), along with fantasies of revenge, stubbornness, self-pity, and loss of control. This is true for individuals and for nations. What memory keeps alive isn't a single emotion but a complex of tangled experiences. So if you somehow get over one aspect, you've only defused a single ingredient; many more remain active, keeping the whole chemistry of anger boiling. It's amazing to people how glimpsing an old spouse, or the mention of his name, or seeing on a restaurant menu some food he liked to eat, is enough to bring back everything. How can the whole past return so swiftly after so much time?

The way the mind works, it takes only one fragment to resurrect the past. The whole is contained in every part. If you are still mad as hell today over things that happened years ago, you have left the door open to a complete system of interconnected memories. The key words are psychologically murky, yet they apply to all of us when we are haunted by memory:

unresolved feelings

crucial events

personal relationships

winning and losing

gains and losses

unwanted change

forced decisions

regrets

unfulfilled desires

Any of these components can reactivate the whole system, drawing you back into a given picture of reality. Take one especially loaded item: personal relationships. For many people all it takes is a word like *mother* or *father* to cause a complex, highly emotional gestalt to arise. Suddenly you are five and being spanked for something your brother did. Suddenly it's your wedding day and your mother is acting cold and distant instead of being happy for you. Or perhaps no single image comes to mind; they all conflate into a feeling-state that makes you weak, confused, and upset.

A trivial incident brought all of this home to a friend of mine. Some years before the conflict in Bosnia flared up, she had traveled as a tourist to the beautiful Dalmatian coast of the former Yugoslavia. "Looking out our bus window, everything looked ancient—timeless cobbled streets and churches, towns that seemed to have grown naturally from the rugged rocky coast. After a few days I fell into a kind of idyllic haze, imagining how peaceful a place this must be. Then one night as we were going to a restaurant, the tour guide, who was Serbian, picked up the microphone at the front of the bus and said, 'Please don't walk around on the streets alone. I just saw some Albanians.'

"My husband and I stared at each other. Albanians? They weren't people we had any fear of; in fact they weren't people we had any opinion about. But to this young woman the word implied some ingrained suspicion and fear. She had no idea that it was almost funny to us that the boogeyman was an Albanian, but to her it "was very real." Soon enough the world would see the persecution of ethnic Albanians in Kosovo as the news networks carried images of fleeing refugees, tent cities erected at the border, and tales of Serbian militias ruthlessly burning and pillaging villages and farms. Memory fueled destruction, because a story was too old to forget.

The same mechanism that keeps an ancient ethnic grudge alive operates in us as individuals. We buy into a picture of reality that shuts out new information and new experiences. We let anger color innocent details of life. We trap old rages inside until they fester. Behind the simple word *Albanian,* hidden processes were lurking, and the outbreak of violence proved it.

The way of peace asks us not to wait for such outbreaks. Even though our egos struggle to keep memories intact, life wants to change the picture in a dynamic, fluid way. It's not true to this flow for any picture to remain stuck. The chemistry of anger can be very persuasive, yet at the same time something stronger pulls us toward healing and growth, toward integrating old hurts and new experiences.

War has to be understood as a very powerful gestalt, its existence deeply buried inside us. Yet the way of peace offers the mind a new picture that will satisfy it. Its key words are:

connection
mature love
love of self
inner strength
fulfilled desires
achievement
giving
inspiration
vision

In modern America, even a war president has to offer at least the semblance of these qualities, which is tremendously hopeful. On the surface the war gestalt still seems all-powerful, and by calling on national unity, defense of the homeland, belligerence against the enemy, and all the other tried-and-true values of war making, a politician can intimidate anyone who opposes him by accusing them of being unpatriotic.

But in truth this strategy has lost a lot of steam. A war president can no longer motivate a nation with certain time-honored values because they are now outdated: conquest, desire for expansion, imperial glory, and manifest destiny used to justify violence against another country, and there was little disagreement over them. The Spanish-American War of 1898 was fueled by this brand of rhetoric, as were the wars against the Indians in the West, following the tradition of conquest that had held sway, with minor changes, since Columbus landed four centuries earlier.

The second war in Iraq provoked suspicion that a desire for conquest is still America's prime motivation. But what I find encouraging is the degree to which the language of peace infiltrated that particular war.

Connection: America's stated purpose was to bring the Iraqis into the community of free nations, connecting them with the modern world and ending their isolation.

Mature love: The U.S. government asserted emotional solidarity with those in Iraq who want freedom and democracy; we asserted compassion for the victims of a repressive regime.

Love of self: Americans felt proud and confident about their identity and believed all other people share this self-love.

Inner strength: American leaders declared their willingness to do the right thing, staying the course even if external circumstances turned against us.

Achievement: Toppling the regime of Saddam Hussein, whatever the final cost, was considered a historic achievement by the war planners.

Giving: America saw itself as sacrificing lives and treasure for an altruistic end.

Inspiration: Bringing democracy to the Middle East was supposed to inspire political change throughout the entire region.

Vision: The ultimate vision behind the war was one of democracy and freedom for all peoples around the world.

One is startled to find that values which belong so clearly to the way of peace are serving the purpose of war, but such is the ambiguity of our time. An American leader has to call upon a vision of national unity that is based on goodness, despite the fact that this goodness spells horrific loss of life and this unity incites a large part of the population to feel enraged. Don't imagine that I am condoning war. The way of peace is never through war, but in a time of transition, one can sense how hard everyone is struggling to hold two opposite pictures together at the same time. We are being good to kill the citizens we are liberating. We are being good to repair the electricity and water supplies we destroyed.

Orwellian logic can't last forever. Eventually the tangled hierarchy has to shift, then we will find ourselves accepting a picture of peace as being natural, right, and politically sound. I believe that a majority of Americans cannot form a picture of war in their minds and live comfortably with it. This is one of the symptoms of a major shift in worldview.

There is no meaning to the world except that which human beings assign to it. This is one of the laws of spirit that conforms to the laws of biology. The brain is faced every day with the same challenge: how to make sense of the four billion bits of sensory data that bombard it every minute. It doesn't compile reality one piece at a time, the way you assemble a jigsaw puzzle on a table, searching for scattered elements out of a jumble of fragments. The mind works in exactly the opposite way: Once it makes a picture of reality, everything is coaxed into a meaning that fits that picture.

If you wave the Confederate flag in downtown Atlanta (or the Nazi flag in downtown Berlin, or a picture of Zapata in downtown Mexico City) people will react to a story that is old but still alive for them. Yet the symbol will change as new eyes look at it and new people respond to it from their ongoing life stories.

The future has a life of its own, because human beings *are* the mystery that lies at its heart. The X factor lives inside us, and if we want to, we can direct this mystery with our will. The entire operation occurs within the brain, and once we understand more about such basic operations as memory, will, intelligence, and intention, world peace will be closer at hand. Consider an event that once made you angry (or humiliated or frightened) but that you now barely remember. What is it that caused you to let go?

THE CHEMISTRY OF CHANGE

Working free of bad memories

I found new ways to be happy.
I learned to forgive.
I stopped looking at my old hurt.
I no longer depend on somebody else to solve my problems.
I gained a new vision.
I took the vision seriously.
I found a deeper sense of self.
I have an expanded sense of self.

The difference between a haunting memory and one that loses its charge over time is this: If a memory becomes part of your identity, forgetting it is extremely difficult. However, if a memory doesn't shape your sense of who you are, you can forget it fairly easily. War and violence have become part of our identity. Admitting that is very important, because it makes all the other steps more urgent. The alternative is to remain trapped by the memories that war has forced each of us to accept. War is not out there happening to other people far away. It is an extension of our personal feelings and our personal memories here and now. So here is how to forget war by embracing the here and now:

Finding new ways to be happy

Unhappy people are always confused when they are told to try and be happy. Their minds are occupied by grievances; there seems to be no room for new experiences that might be uplifting, and even if they came along, they would be seen through the gray haze of one's misery. So the search cannot be for happy experiences. Those are already available in abundance. The search is for an opening that allows happiness to *become* your experience. This opening comes about very differently from the way most people suppose. Most people try to make themselves happy by forcing their unhappy feelings underground, or by turning their backs on them or pretending that they don't exist.

If you have a closet stuffed with junk, the best way to find room for new stuff is to clean the closet. In this case the closet is the nervous system, and one cleans it out at the level of awareness.

The healing process isn't mystical; it involves well-known practical steps.

Look directly at what hurts you.
Communicate your desire to be free of this hurt.
Ask for inner guidance to show you what to do.
Listen to what you feel, but don't give in to it.

Know for certain that you can remove old hurts.

Be patient, since you will have to return to your old hurt many
times.

Most people feel trapped by their resentments because their
behavior runs counter to these steps. They don't look honestly at
their hurt but focus instead on blaming someone outside themselves. They don't communicate a desire to let go of their anger
but keep nursing it. Instead of listening to what they feel in the
moment, they replay the same tired reactions from the past.
Instead of being patient, they take a few random stabs at healing
only to conclude that there's nothing to be done.

Nations do the same thing, which is why peace negotiations
fail so often; nobody is really taking on the steps of healing that
could succeed. The process I've just described works for angry
nations and for angry people. A hundred years of therapy has
established that the mechanism of healing is real; it only needs to
be tried.

Learning to forgive

The emphasis here is on the word *learning*. The reason that people
cannot forgive is that their anger has worn a deep groove in the
mind, and like water seeking a downward slope, their minds find
this groove so easily that new channels of feeling cannot be
formed. Forgiveness is a feeling. We are used to thinking of it as a
moral duty or as a sign of maturity. True as those things may be,
if you cannot feel the experience of forgiving, you haven't
achieved the real thing.

Learning to make a new groove for your feelings is the key.
Once again, the steps aren't mystical. You can forgive anyone
who has hurt you by taking the following actions:

Choose the intent to forgive, even though your feelings are
still hurt.

Have the intention to let new feelings come in.

Encourage even the slightest hints of new feeling.

Experience the old hurt and anger, but always say, This isn't
me. This is not what I want anymore.

Keep challenging the old hurt with reasons why it should be
replaced.

Be patient and let yourself experience both the old and the
new feelings until the old one begins to fade.

This process is very similar to the one I described for making yourself happy when you feel burdened by misery. In both cases you will be working within yourself, privately but not alone. Unhappiness is solitary; healing is not. That's because your rage and hurt depend entirely on your personal history. It took specific people to create the memory that haunts you.

Healing is bigger than personality. When someone gets a cut, we don't say, *Maybe his skin will heal, who knows? It all depends on the kind of person he is.* Your skin heals independently of who you are. Psychological healing works exactly the same way. You don't have to be nice, good, smart, or deserving. Yet how many of us secretly believe that we should continue to suffer because we deserve to, or because we aren't nice enough, good enough, or smart enough to change?

The big difference between healing the skin and healing the mind is that you have to participate in the latter. But this difference is not a stumbling block once the healing gets under way. At the level of the soul there lies an entire healing mechanism every bit as effective as the body's immune system. If you have the intention to heal, you give new energy permission to come into you and clear away obstacles, which is exactly what happened to my friend Jean.

Jean grew up in a military family with a father who demanded discipline from all his children, including the only girl. Because there were four boys surrounding her, Jean felt that she became one of the troops, as her father liked to call his children. She gravitated to her mother, which was a saving grace, but early in adolescence Jean discovered that she had trouble with boyfriends.

"I felt incredibly insecure, and I made the mistake of throwing myself emotionally at any boy who gave the slightest hint of liking me. I rebelled against my parents and stayed out late, no surprise considering my father's strict rules. But I was also reckless sexually, and finally things culminated in an abortion at seventeen. My mother was deeply ashamed, and we both agreed to keep the abortion a secret from my father.

"It was another ten years and one divorce later before I confronted what was happening inside me. My anger against my father was obvious. We rarely talked; I kept my distance, and since he had always been unavailable, that seemed to suit him just fine. My mother was no help, and my own feelings of rage, which seemed totally right and justified, kept saying to me, *Why bother to change? He deserves everything.*

"For some reason this argument stopped working after twenty-seven years. I can't exactly say what the turning point was. I just managed to make a tiny shift, and when I did, I saw that the only person being harmed by my suffering was me. From that point on it wasn't easy. I had to face my own wounds, using any number of friends and therapists along the way. It took ten years, but I knew I would never be at peace until I faced these demons.

"The day never came when I sat up in bed and said, *Oh, I'm over it.* But bit by bit my world got better. As I broke free from each little demon, people related to me in a more relaxed way. I was more open, less like a cactus you couldn't touch. My mind started to see the world as less threatening; I grew in appreciation. None of these things had a direct bearing on my father. Then one day my mother called to say that my father had just gone to the doctor for a biopsy; they suspected prostate cancer. And the moment I put down the phone, I cried. I was crying for him, and I can say that it was the first time I could do that instead of crying for myself. I had no idea that forgiveness would feel like that. It marked my freedom from the past and the opening of a new life."

No longer looking at the old hurt

Wounds cry out for attention. If they are physical they cry out with physical pain. If they are psychological they cry out with mental anguish. During the healing process your pain is going to linger as long as it needs to. Even so, there is a difference between noticing your pain and dwelling on it. We all know people who will use any excuse to draw attention to themselves, including a fixation on their current woes. The danger is that if you identify with your hurt, if you use it as your calling card, if you think it makes you more sympathetic, all these factors retard healing.

One of the most insidious aspects of anger is that it is so much easier to feel than other emotions. I don't just mean positive emotions like compassion but even negative ones like fear, anxiety, uncertainty, and self-doubt. Anger is also socially acceptable. Athletes use it to motivate themselves, for instance, and sometimes a football victory seems more like a battle won than the outcome of a game.

The way of peace asks you to make a fine distinction. Be aware of your hurt and pay attention to it. But do not fixate on it. This can be a difficult distinction to honor. There will always be moments when you can't tell if you are letting go of a hurt by expressing it, or just venting. The difference comes down to intention. If you vent anger with the object of spreading your toxic feelings, the result will have nothing to do with healing. Your anger is your weapon. On the other hand, if you release anger the way you'd expel a rock from your shoe, your intention clearly has healing behind it. Once the anger starts flowing, both of these alternatives might feel the same. Anger is anger. But if you have a healing intention, two things will happen: you will feel more peaceful after your anger has been released, and you will feel like an old, fixed belief in enemies and injustice has started to move.

No longer depending on others

Hurts isolate us. When you suffer, you suffer privately, no matter how close someone else may be to you. Some people react to this isolation by becoming even more alone. They nurse their grievances in silence. They gain a sense of strength from toughing it out alone. Other people react in the opposite way, wanting to pull as many people into their suffering as possible.

Both tactics defy the first law of healing, which is that it must occur within yourself. This isn't the same as going it alone or toughing it out. That's the ego's interpretation, and if you look a bit deeper, you'll find that what's really going on is resistance. The ego is saying, *I don't deserve to have this happen. I'm going to sit tight until someone notices and takes pity on me.*

We all have ego reactions, and they must be overcome. If you face them for what they are, temporary energies that block your true self, you will realize that calling on your true self—the soul, higher consciousness, deeper awareness—will begin to move these obstacles out of the way. When you gain access to your true self, even a little bit, you will begin to feel connected once again.

Of course other people can be a comfort and a help along the way. As you reconnect with yourself, you will reconnect with other people spontaneously since they are a mirror of your self. But depending on others to solve your problems never works, because even though you may feel connected to them, you are really reaching out as one ego to another. Healing doesn't take place at the level of ego, however, and no matter how much sympathy and agreement you are surrounded by, no matter how many people tell you that you are right, you haven't removed the blocks that keep new life from rushing in to heal you.

Slave owners in the Old South had lots of friends who sympathized with all the woes of managing slaves, getting them to perform on command, facing the threats of potential escapes and rebellions. The fact that everyone in the social system agrees with you doesn't make your actions right, however; in this case the fact that a slave owner believed he could own another human being was a form of profound ignorance about reality and the self. In our present circumstances, it's easy to find a group that agrees wholeheartedly that war is right, that the enemy is evil, that soldiers carry the burden of keeping the peace and must be supported at all costs. The way of peace doesn't attack this mindset, but it also doesn't shrink from the truth that it needs to be healed inside each person.

Gaining a new vision

We live immersed in so much information that new ways of seeing things are widely available. In any sizable American city you can go to a library or bookstore to immerse yourself in Tibetan Buddhism, Sufism, esoteric Christianity, or the teachings of countless sages and saints. Everything is available all the time.

How, then, do you attain a way of seeing things that isn't just a momentary enthusiasm? The vision becomes yours when you can see yourself in it. By this I don't mean that you see yourself as a finished product. A vision isn't about the future. It's about taking on what is truly yours, right here and now. If transformation doesn't take place every day, it is little more than an ideal that always lies just over the horizon.

If your vision keeps you on the move, then it's a true vision. For me, the way of peace is true because I find myself with change every day. Unfortunately, many people choose a vision that is guaranteed to never challenge them or create change. Religions are particularly susceptible to this, because you can be among the faithful and still know who you should hate, who worships God in the wrong way, who is a sinner and devoid of any need for compassion.

A vision that makes you choose fixed sides isn't a vision. I can't put it any more baldly than that. You may run across a spiritual system that really appeals to you, but after a while you notice that you still feel resentful and limited; you notice that the whole system seems to be about belonging to a tight, closed group; you are asked to direct your life in some right way instead of the wrong way. These are all symptoms that tell you to leave. A true vision never demands that you do the right thing. It never condemns outsiders for their ignorance and sin. Our egos already know how to do these things very well; we don't need a spiritual vision to support the very habits that need to change.

Finding a deeper sense of self

Language throws little traps our way all the time. One of them snaps shut whenever we use words like *higher self, deeper self,* or *true self.* They sound like innocent, even helpful phrases, but there is actually only one self, and it's the one you are experiencing right now. You can't get off the stage and go somewhere deeper, higher, or truer to find a different self. Everything that will ever happen to the self appears on the screen of your mind in the same way that wanting a hamburger, remembering your name, or fantasizing about a beach in Bermuda shows up. The show that hits the screen is filled with thoughts, feelings, hopes, dreams, fantasies, and impulses of every kind.

Yet there is something else behind the screen, and that is where transformation comes in.

The screen is two-dimensional, whether you project a cheap cartoon on it or the greatest painting in the history of art. And yet the great painting suggests a third dimension. It makes you feel as if you are touched by beauty, by genius, by inspiration, nobility, even God.

These feelings that leak through the limitations of the mental screen are also leaking through the world of everyday events. It's as if what lies behind the screen wants to get your attention, and the only way it can is by leaking through physical reality. In order to grow spiritually, you don't have to start out with a good self-image, but it is necessary to have one that is porous. Spirit has to be able to soak into it. It has to be flexible enough to let you know when you are touched by beauty and truth. If your self-image is inflexible, it hardly matters whether it is good or bad. Smugness and self-importance are just as impervious to spirit as shame and fear. We've all been touched by cheap sentiment and unmoved by great art. It's not the truth of what you look at, it's the truth of how you look. The secret lies in the act of perceiving. Being moved by a child in trouble can bring violence to an end if the right person sees that child; a lifetime of seeing murder on television isn't enough to end a single act of violence if the perceiver is closed off.

The key is a willingness to be touched, over and over and over. I know people who come out of a disturbing movie grumbling, "I didn't like the characters. The whole thing brought me down. I don't need to pay money to feel bad." These closed-off attitudes are acceptable to the soul. In every audience someone will also be openly touched. As long as that capacity is alive, one's connection with spirit is getting stronger. The only people I worry about are those who say, "I already know what I know. I don't need to see this again. What else is new?" They seem to be immune to the depth of life and can only access flat images that flicker without feeling across the screen of the mind.

Having an expanded sense of self

Any new identity that you find on your life's journey is going to morph into another identity as you continue along. All these identities can be healthy, yet it's undeniable that to grow from one identity to the next involves destruction. The habits of the old self must give way to the habits of the new.

Nature manages this act of destruction with as little pain as possible. If we can imagine what happens as a two-year-old turns into a three-year-old, we will be looking at the most natural and painless way of transformation. What does nature do? Think back to yourself as a growing child. The process is so subtle that hardly anyone notices.

Nature let you be who you are.

It didn't burden you with projecting prematurely into the future.

It didn't hold you back in the past.

It gave you new desires.

These new desires led you in the right direction.

If you can evolve spiritually in just this way, you have found the truest path, regardless of the teacher or belief system you choose. As a child you weren't aware of the mystery of change. You did the things that came naturally to a two-year-old, and when the time came to become a three-year-old, new desires arose. As parents we stand back and marvel at this metamorphosis, yet we don't apply it to ourselves. Instead we concoct a scheme for forced change, motivated by hating the ugly parts of ourselves, feeling insecure and inadequate, wanting anything but whatever is right before us.

If you find a spiritual teacher or guide who reinforces these negative feelings, I'm afraid you are moving in the wrong direction. I realize that there are tough, demanding spiritual disciplines. They ask you to spend nights in the cold sleeping on a wooden floor, or fighting your ego to the death, denying your lower self and all its sinful impulses. But the way of peace isn't so demanding. Its *discipline* simply means constancy, patience, and renewed trust in what is real as opposed to self-delusion.

The reality is that you can be a beacon of consciousness. Whatever mistake you have made about who you are is temporary. Your true identity has remained untouched. You have never sinned against it or affected it in any way except to lose touch with it. The prevailing problem for each person is separation and nothing else. So any path that wants you to change yourself must keep in mind that there is no self to change. There are only masks that we wear for a moment and then discard. If you can cherish yourself even as you discard your current favorite mask, you are living perfectly in the way of peace.

WHY DOES GOD
WANT WAR?

TODAY I AM restless with frustration. I've just finished debating with four religious leaders on *Larry King Live*, but I couldn't see their faces because they were all in the U.S. while I was stuck in a cramped TV studio in Quito, Ecuador. A good place not to believe what I was hearing.

"There will never be peace on earth until the Prince of Peace returns," a buzzing, crackling voice said in my ear piece. The Southern Baptist. "We're all sinners. God knows that. God tells us that in revelation. You can't have peace when everybody is a sinner." The Southern Baptist had a lot more to say about sin. I squirmed and waited.

The next buzzing sounded like angry hornets. "It's preposterous to blame religion for war," droned a different voice. "Religious wars have killed barely a fraction of what such godless murderers as Hitler and Stalin have done. We must have religion, or we would be killing each other all the time." That was the Jewish radio talk show host. I squirmed some more. *What are we doing here, comparing our ideas of acceptable slaughter?* I pushed the point that religion has been responsible for wars throughout history, and didn't Hitler mention God quite a lot?

The hornets got really riled. "No, no. Without religion the world would be much worse off. It's through God that we remember to love one another. Fathers and mothers. Husbands and wives." Ah, the benign Catholic priest. All that Baptist talk about sin must have gotten to him. He wants to make sure we all hear about Christ's love. It was sad how tired he sounded, as if beating the drum for love wasn't going to work, and he knew it.

The voices clamored on, and I had no choice but to squirm, because I realized after five minutes that not a single one of them was going to offer a way to end war. It was depressing. They were all on the show basically for one reason: to shout, murmur, argue, convince, harangue, and intimate that their religion was better than anyone else's. The Muslim, whose voice was the quietest (he knew he was licked from the start), had to practice patience while the others all but sneered openly at his warrior faith. Not that anybody was going to shake him. In its darkest hour he was as sure of the superiority of Islam as they were of their home teams.

The last word was left to the Jewish talk show guy, who was feeling a burst of camaraderie. "See? Only in America could we all sit down like friends, all from different faiths, to talk like this." Oh, really? He seemed to think the state police would have broken things up in Sweden or Holland or some other hotbed of intolerance.

So now the show's over, and the pretty, smiling girl from the Quito TV station is pulling out my earpiece. I'm giving another talk in another country tomorrow, so it's off to bed. I trudge into the warm equatorial night. Why fret about our mini-council of faith? It's not like God is going to speak out against our violent conflicts down here.

Yet part of the anguish of war comes from religion's total

failure to end it. Every religion teaches that killing is absolutely wrong. One cannot love God without loving and cherishing other human beings. Religion exists to make us face our violence and greed, and then to overcome those qualities. As someone once beautifully put it, religion plants a seed in our open wounds, and from that seed a tree of peace will grow.

Which makes the fact that religion doesn't do that all the more tragic. At the present moment religion is dead for millions of people, and rightly so. They attend church for its comforting rituals or because it is the right thing to do, but long ago they realized, as any sensible person would, that churches do little or nothing to bring the problem of war to an end. God himself seems to have no concern about our deep suffering. He has been reduced to a remote, aged grandparent wringing his hands on the sidelines as his children kill each other. In Michael Moore's polemical film *Fahrenheit 9/11,* the most wrenching scene centers on a mother in Flint, Michigan, who first appears as a supporter of the Iraq War.

This support is based not on animosity toward Arabs but on a sense of morality. She points out that working-class people in a town like Flint, which is bedrock working-class, always do what's right when it comes to patriotism. One reads in her eyes the convictions of an upstanding churchgoer, a conservative Republican, and an upholder of family values. By a heartbreaking twist of fate, she also becomes one of the thousand mothers who has lost a child in combat. The son she was proud to send to war is snatched from her, and the next time we meet her, grief has destroyed every conviction that led her to defend the war.

No longer the staunch patriot, she is now bitter about what she sees as lies and deceit that led to the invasion of Iraq. She agonizes over the cruelty of fate that took an innocent life. She suffers over the unnatural act of a mother burying a child when it should be the other way around. Finally, we see her in Washington, D.C., at a professional conference. Hoping that a visit to the White House might restore her strength, or at least bring some solace, she finds the opposite. The sight of the White House causes her to stumble and then collapse in grief, mumbling the wrenching words, "I didn't think it would be this hard."

Consider what religion has done to every person like her. It has convinced her that authority is always right, that a common person's duty is to fall into line without questions or doubts. It has taught her that people who protest authority are bad and wrong (she explicitly tells us about her repugnance toward the anti-war movement). It has taught her that God is on the side of a good war, which is the only kind America ever fights.

And what didn't it teach her? Religion didn't teach her about how to confront the darkest side of human nature so that it can be transformed. It didn't teach her to think for herself in spiritual matters. It didn't teach her to forgive and tolerate potential enemies. Most of all, it didn't teach her the true nature of God, for religion grossly betrays the truth when it portrays God as a rigid authority with military instincts and a liking for bloodshed.

Someone may protest that I don't know this woman and have never been to her church. Yet it isn't hard to read between the lines. Witnessing the state of helpless grief and confusion into which this mother fell, I find it unquestionable that religion has failed her. Religion has put God on the side of war for the following reasons:

WHY GOD SUPPORTS WAR

The truth must be defended.

Unholy acts defile God and must be punished.

Heresy is a crime that true believers must redress.

Vengeance is part of God's nature.

Sometimes a lesser evil is needed to vanquish a greater evil.

Human beings must struggle to find God, even to the point of
struggling in war.

God doesn't interfere in human affairs and has sent no sign
that he opposes war.

Centuries ago, in an age of faith, all these reasons would have
made perfect sense. Now, however, they sound disturbing and
false. What sensible person would kill someone else because
heretics and unbelievers must not succeed? Is it really credible
that God would label one side alone as purely wicked, making it
clear to the faithful that they are on the side without sin? Reading
God's mind is an act of arrogance, an illusion of the ego. The
obvious fact that God doesn't interfere in human affairs makes it
impossible to assert that he favors war. God doesn't intrude, because human affairs are our responsibility. God transcends war
altogether. The deity allows us to wage war on our own, which to
those who want war in the first place indicates tacit approval.

The argument that war is part of a larger spiritual struggle is
more unusual. I've heard it voiced in fatalistic terms, as proof
that sin is universal and leads to violence. As born sinners we are
fated to fight until our final redemption. But the same argument
is encountered in a subtler New Age version. Some spiritual
teachers describe the journey toward enlightenment as a kind
of inner war. Every breakthrough is won by struggling against
obstacles that have been thrown up by karma or the ego. Make no
mistake, I once heard a teacher say, "your ego will never give up
until you have fought it to the death."

But I think the reason most people who worship God are
willing to go to war is that they want to prevent evil. This is the

lesser evil argument, and it found a perfect model in World War II, which is constantly referred to as a good war because allowing the Nazis to succeed in their plans for a final solution would have been a much greater evil. Pacifism was treated with criminal punishment during the war, and some moralists argue that being a pacifist was tantamount to murder, because if you don't stop wholesale slaughter, you are condoning it. Good wars, however, aren't an acceptable excuse not to end war. The deaths of millions of Jews came after two decades of open anti-Semitism from Hitler that was never addressed by other countries. The concept of the good war is brought up by every aggressor, and if the losers in every historical combat had won, they would inevitably have claimed to be working God's will.

For every such argument that turns God into a supporter of war, there are counter-arguments that sound equally convincing and carry great spiritual weight.

WHY GOD OPPOSES WAR

The nature of God is peaceful.

Killing is a sin.

Human life is sacred.

God abhors violence against his creation.

War betrays our higher nature, the part of ourselves closest to God.

War violates the covenant that makes all God's children equal.

These arguments have not prevented war, but without a doubt they have added to the sense that we are sinful and guilty creatures. Thus religion betrays its mission to make God's will into our own. Instead of transforming war into peace, religion nags at our conscience. The good war is on God's side, yet that doesn't erase the sin of murder that war entails. We are promised that God will send sinners to Hell, but isn't that the same as killing the killers? Why does God get to commit the very sin he is punishing?

There is a built-in contradiction here and no nice way out of it. You can invent a circular logic in which sinners keep committing murder and then turning to God for forgiveness, a cycle that never ends, or else you can give God a split personality, as I was brought up to do, assigning him one face of creation and love, another of destruction and death. The schism between Jehovah and Christ exhibits this either/or tendency, as does the split between Krishna and Shiva.

The way of peace doesn't claim that God must be a pacifist. The gulf between pacifist and warmonger belongs in our psychology, not in the nature of God. Divine schizophrenia can be overcome by seeing certain spiritual truths and holding on to them.

God isn't a person.

We cannot read his mind.

The essence of God is consciousness.

Consciousness can be used for either violence or peace; the choice is ours.

When it is expanded, human consciousness chooses nonviolence since that is compatible with love.

If these principles are valid, then God doesn't have to jump into the middle of human affairs. He stands for the pure essence of life and love. For me to solve my personal anguish over war, I must transform my consciousness until violence is no longer an option. By now this is a familiar argument. Millions of people understand it. Why should religion hold back?

It shouldn't. It doesn't have to. If any religion would make the same choice to join the way of peace that individuals are making every day, faith would be a living force once again. What kind of changes does this entail? You already know them as they apply to you, but let's be explicit:

Religion must place the responsibility for violence squarely where it belongs, in the mind of every person.

It must stop judging others outside the faith as sinners condemned by God.

It must stop defending war in any way.

It must stop claiming to be the one and only path to God.

It must give up its arrogance and claim to authority.

It must renounce its covert greed and desire for power.

It must discover how to return love to its true place of primacy.

These changes may not occur in our lifetime, but we cannot pretend that they are merely optional. Nor are they the grumblings of an enemy of the church. I attended religious schools for years while growing up. I have been moved by my parents' deep religious beliefs. My mother went to temple at dawn every day to pray to Rama; my father was buried according to Hindu rites that date back thousands of years. I probably have rooted my identity in religion more deeply than the average person who considers himself an upholder of traditional values. But I am also a modern person, and what I've witnessed since the days of my religious upbringing is too obvious to ignore: the views that dominate our current understanding of human nature have rendered religion irrelevant.

These new views are basically scientific, and they explain violence in totally nonreligious ways. In medical school I became a convert to science, and I know the beliefs that dominate scientific thinking to be very powerful. One belief, initiated by Sigmund Freud, is that we get our violence from the unconscious. In this view there is a dark realm inside everyone, what Carl Jung called the shadow. In this realm lie atavistic impulses of rage and fear. In daily life we don't contact the shadow; we pretend it doesn't exist, and unfortunately that attitude makes us its slaves. When wars break out, the shadow rises to the surface and wreaks havoc.

The psychological view of violence renders religion irrelevant because we can only escape enslavement to the shadow by exploring it, bringing in the light of consciousness. Exploring the shadow turns religious people off. They prefer to live with the drama of sin and redemption, where the lines are clear cut: you do wrong, God condemns you; you do right, God rewards you. Basically, this is the relationship of a child to a parent. In the family setting reward and punishment work, since children need to be taught the lessons of right and wrong. When extended to adulthood, the weaknesses are glaring. An adult who leaves morality to a parental God has abdicated his responsibility to be an active agent for good. An adult who thinks that hidden impulses of rage and fear are innate sin is abdicating her responsibility to root out darkness. War and violence stem from the awareness of each and every person. At their core all religions say this, and when religion is used as a way to avoid self-confrontation, it has died.

The second prevailing viewpoint about why violence exists is genetic. Genetics is based on the Darwinian laws of survival. If a trait helps a species to survive, it persists and becomes part of its genetic makeup. If a trait makes a species weaker, limiting its ability to survive, that trait disappears, taking its genes with it. Violence, therefore, has no moral meaning. In our past we had to kill or be killed. Men had to violently seize their mates away from competing males; they all probably violently raped the women they wanted. Various tribes had to win wars against other tribes that coveted their land, food, and women.

Genetics renders religion irrelevant because in its view we are animals, an offshoot of the primate family along with gorillas and chimpanzees. We've already touched on this perspective. Since the genes of *Homo sapiens* are only one percent different from the genes of gorillas, the argument seems irrefutable, and by now people are so convinced by it that to compare us to angels seems nothing but sentimentality. Hamlet is the most despairing and suicidal of any great literary hero, yet he says of human beings, "In form how like an angel, in apprehension how like a god!" Genetics would soberly point out that in form we are only a few steps ahead of Neanderthals, and probably in apprehension, too.

Religion might not be perishing of its own internal failings without science, but with science against it, there is not much hope. Freud's breakthrough dates back a century, Darwin's a century and a half. The intervening period has rendered religion increasingly untrustworthy. Our task today is to restore hope by doing one of two things. They happen to be opposites:

1. Keep on defending traditional religion to the last ditch, no matter how much it contradicts reason.
2. Urge religion to evolve so that it gains the kind of relevance that science cannot defeat.

Although it may seem that religious people have chosen the first alternative in overwhelming numbers, I think appearances are deceiving. People of spiritual intent have been finding new ways to think about God; they have looked to quantum physics to explain reality in such a way that miracles and the existence of the soul are even more credible than they were in traditional religion. Spirit has returned, not as blind obedience to a canon, but as a personal exploration of consciousness. We still ask the same age-old questions about who we are and where we came from. The same age-old answers, that we are spiritual beings who came from God, return to us, only now the path has been walked with open eyes and an expanded mind, not rigid adherence to dogma.

And what about war? God can show us how to evolve out of our present anguish by retracing the steps that drew us into it. God shows the way through consciousness, because God *is* consciousness. If your mind feels conflicted, or guilty, or schizoid, there is no other way to view God than through those lenses. If your mind is organized, coherent, and clear, there is no other way to view God than through those lenses. You cannot escape one basic fact: at any given stage of personal evolution, you are seeing reality as yourself. The biblical story of how God created man in his own image isn't complete until we realize that man returned the favor by creating God in his image, too.

There are as many versions of God as there are people in the world. However, these can be simplified into seven stages that match the seven stages of consciousness. They are like glasses that give us a certain viewpoint on the world. As evolution proceeds, God changes. The level of consciousness that makes God a supporter of war and a source of fear shifts, to be replaced by a peaceful and loving God. That God is only sustainable, however, if your awareness has shifted to support it. This is one of the laws that govern spirituality. As you evolve, so will the divine. The way of peace depends on bringing that truth to life, step by step.

GOD IS REVEALED IN STAGES

Stage 1: Chaos, Conflict, War

IN THE LEAST evolved stage of God, he or she presides over a world of unpredictable disasters. Human beings confront nature in the raw, including their own nature. A world of beasts attacking and feeding off each other is translated into a society where man is the wolf and also the prey. Behavior is atavistic, a throwback to the primitive physical choice presented by fight-or-flight.

When someone is in stage one, the tangled hierarchy is dominated by the following:

fear
random events
blind reactions
fight-or-flight
enemies everywhere
oppression
depression
sinfulness

This stage of consciousness creates tremendous uncertainty, as attested to by the days after 9/11. The American public felt waves of shock and fear. Terror created the potential for chaos, and the solution was to organize and fight. That shift was embodied by Mayor Rudolph Giuliani, who responded with great eloquence on the first day, drawing the public together through an honest reaction of deep dismay—he spoke of casualties too great for the heart to bear. As time passed, Giuliani became a militant hardliner against terrorism, calling for any sacrifice to defeat it.

Leaders must show that they don't share in the public's fear, so they overreact by seizing power and control. Their knee-jerk reaction is to withhold freedom from an entire society, because evildoers flourish wherever there is too much freedom. This claim is the opposite of the truth, but that is ignored. (As I write, in the aftermath of the terrorist attack on the school in Beslan, Russia's President Putin has predictably called for more governmental power, a harsher crackdown on the enemy, and a tougher attitude of militancy, just as President George W. Bush did after the September 11 attacks in 2001.)

In this stage God mirrors these fearful attitudes. He is harsh and unyielding. He condemns his enemies, against whom he wants absolute vengeance. It would be a mistake to identify him as totally an Old Testament God, although Jehovah does display all these characteristics. Even Christ is given a handful of passages about sinners being thrown into the abyss with wailing and gnashing of teeth.

As in every stage of consciousness, God must fit the world that he has created. Thus a world of random and unpredictable disasters calls forth a capricious, willful God. He must be feared and placated to keep him from unleashing his vengeance. We beg to be saved from our sins, yet we expect the worst, since sin never really gets abolished, and we therefore deserve anything that happens.

But the chaos that people so deeply fear is actually internal. It exists in our awareness, and trying to project it onto our enemies doesn't work. The war on terrorism is bound to fail, because if all you choose to see is enemies everywhere, you will be fated to have an ever-replenishing crop of enemies.

This first stage ends when consciousness shifts. There is an inner contradiction in a God who creates disasters and then expects us to worship him as the answer to our fears. Isn't he also the source of our fears? The unworkable tactic in this stage is to conquer fear by turning it into anger. The magical transformation from fear to anger lies behind every military response. Armies embody a desire to be tough, defended, strong, and aggressive. That stance seems like the opposite of fear, which makes a person feel weak, undefended, and out of control. But only when fear is actually confronted for what it is, can it be defused. At that point stage one comes to an end, and God acquires a new face.

Stage 2: Law, Order, Achievement

IN THE NEXT stage God presides over a world of law. Chaos from stage one has given way to order. We look out upon a world where nature remains within bounds, governed by its own predictable principles. This is a more benign world, calling forth a more benign God. I might call him the business-as-usual God. He appears in the Old Testament after the catastrophe of Adam and Eve being expelled from the Garden of Eden. They are under a terrible curse, yet normal life must go on. So the Bible begins its recitation of the many laws that are to govern civil life, beginning with the Ten Commandments but soon expanding into hundreds of precepts. God becomes interested in providing a good life, a virtuous life, for his children.

In stage two the tangled hierarchy is dominated by the following:

organization
orderliness
cooperation
laws
money
civil society
competition
free markets

None of these are religious words, yet they infuse every spiritual tradition. The laws of Manu in India parallel the laws of Moses.

Both provide a scheme for human beings to live together so that something solid can be achieved. This is the stage where war becomes rational, a means to get more land, money, and power. People still live in fear, but it is hidden behind the mask of business as usual. God is no longer so capricious (his last Biblical act of taunting human beings comes in the Book of Job, which begins with Jehovah betting Satan that a virtuous man cannot have his faith broken through trials of unspeakable misery. Jehovah isn't on the wrong side of the bet, but he is just as manipulative as Satan). God allows himself to be bound up in laws; one no longer has to guess what he wants. This is obviously a human need more than a divine one, and it serves society very well.

But order isn't the same as love or forgiveness. If we transgress against God's laws we deserve punishment, sometimes unto death. So there is no resolution of either anger or fear yet. In a contest with raw nature, human beings will always be afraid of being destroyed. They are equally afraid to stand before a judge, human or divine, who has the same power.

The contradiction built into stage two is that violence and order can't coexist without tension. The most rational societies continue to go to war; they just develop more efficient ways to create destruction. The God of stage two may want his children to have a good life, but he is completely comfortable with violence.

At this stage war remains an option, but a dangerous one if it puts a nation's prosperity in peril. Leaders are therefore forced to pretend that wars don't really cost what they cost, that prosperity and war might even go hand in hand.

The unworkable tactic in stage two is materialism, the belief that having enough good things will end suffering. A typical person in stage two might be an educated, middle-class college student getting a deferment from the draft. Education and privilege are called upon as evidence that one is above war. Yet the truth is that wars are an eruption of unconscious drives. As long as these impulses aren't faced, violence has no choice but to persist. One's material status is irrelevant. Poor countries go to war, rich countries go to war. When people face the fact that material success doesn't solve the underlying problem of violence, stage two comes to an end.

Stage 3: Harmony, Nurturing, Inwardness

IN THIS NEXT stage, God is forgiving. He presides over a world that is no longer clouded by the presence of sin. Humans have a better self-image now. The world is a place of harmony, more like a playground than a battlefield. Everything loosens up, and humans begin to explore the possibility that Nature isn't fixed by God. It is evolving; things change and therefore can be made even better.

In stage three the tangled hierarchy is dominated by the following:

looking inward
stability
peace
appreciation
leniency
openness
self-acceptance
non-judgment
nurturing

In this stage it dawns on humans that they are shepherds of the planet. In learning to care for ourselves, we learn to care for

God's creation. God has shifted at the same time in a more benevolent direction. He has lost all desire for vengeance. He sits above the world, happy to let his children pursue their own lives. He is content with having created a harmonious setting for human beings to grow in.

At this stage we look inward because we aren't so afraid of what we might find. The rapacious wolf is gone. There are few inner predators, although there are many shadows and troubling impulses. These aren't enough to disturb our basic sense of being all right; self-acceptance is a new possibility. Self-worth has tipped the balance against sin.

In stage three there is no desire for war. Everything revolves around peace as the normal state of life. Maturity has dawned, and it is seen that peace can only be found by respecting our brothers and sisters and treating them as equals. Societies go into stage three when they are willing to rebuild the ruins of an enemy's country. This is also the stage of morality where one can hate the sin but love the sinner. In other words, a person is allowed to do bad things without being judged as a bad person.

At this stage leaders are peacemakers and humanitarians. Their behavior is no longer competitive or belligerent, but nurturing (Lincoln was nurturing compared to Ulysses S. Grant, Bill Clinton nurturing compared to George W. Bush). Their actions must be consistent with leniency; their policies knit diverse interests together.

The unworkable tactic in stage three centers on the shadow, the hidden part of ourselves that contains a store of rage, fear, and destructiveness from the past. Looking inward always brings out the shadow, but there is no practical way to face it. People in stage three often pretend to be more at peace, more tolerant, and more forgiving than they actually are deep down. They aren't being hypocritical. Rather, the discovery that peace is possible is too cherished to give up, and for most people confronting their inner demons isn't peaceful.

Most societies have now reached the point where a peaceful God is desirable. Evolution has gained this much, even if we tend to slide back into lower stages when the pressures of fear and anger grow too strong. Religions of intolerance are now minority religions; preaching hatred and fear isn't acceptable to the vast majority. Evolution still has a long way to go, though. The God of stage three is not yet fully loving or compassionate; he has not yet welcomed human beings as co-creators of their own reality. Even so, the groundwork has been laid for the next step.

Stage 4: Insight, Conscious Growth, Witnessing

THE GOD OF this stage is a master of revealing hidden truth. He presides over a world layered in mystery. To know God, a person must be willing for the first time to give up materialism, for the gifts of revelation come from unseen layers of reality. They come from what is known in India as the *subtle body* (Shuksham Sharir). I prefer the term *subtle body* to the modern Western notion of the unconscious, because the unconscious implies a place of darkness and blind instinct. The subtle body is wisdom itself, and when a person begins to access it, a flow of insight begins to emerge. The God of stage four is mysterious, but he wants to be known.

In this stage the tangled hierarchy is dominated by the following:

intuition
mystery
inner truth
witnessing

detachment

increased acceptance

self-absorption

God is reflected in the sudden discovery that reality may have its source inside you. The glimmer of this possibility makes the inner world fascinating. Finding your own truth becomes all-important. Since no one can tell you your truth, you become detached from external authority. God in this stage no longer wants to be an authority. He is a hidden presence that reveals itself piece by piece.

On the rare occasion when a deeply insightful person like Vaclav Havel, the first president of a free Czechoslovakia, gains power, there can be extraordinary periods, usually very brief, of national awakening. Gandhi and Lincoln presided over such periods, also, although both had to confront a time of great social turmoil. Leaders at this stage must be completely genuine, complex human beings who have the rare talent to also be a public personage. They govern through their presence, which is felt by those around them as wise, and even saintly.

The God of stage four is worth loving in every respect. He is the essence of understanding. Anyone who feels close to this version of God has achieved a degree of witnessing, the ability to stand outside oneself. Witnessing is detached but not indifferent. People who have come close to death in war or an auto accident speak of the sudden calm that descends on them. However violent the action around them, they feel set apart, as if looking down on the scene from another place. From this place everything is taken care of; there is no resistance to any outside event.

Spirituality becomes much more workable in stage four, because for the first time you are willing to let life run itself. The desperate craving to be in control has loosened its grip. Because you are a witness, you no longer have a mortal stake in everyday affairs. Gain and loss are not opposed; they play their part in a larger design. You begin to see the real possibility of aligning your will with God's will. At this stage war seems foreign and pointless. It can only arise from ignorance, so you set yourself to try and end that ignorance.

The limitation of stage four is that a common solution to war and violence isn't found. As much as you yearn for it, your very detachment from other people makes them less easy to reach. Nor do they relate well to you anymore. You seem uninterested in all their ambitions. You are not a party to their worries. Insight, it turns out, is not enough to change the world.

Stage 5: Creativity, Discovery, Innovation

THE GOD OF this stage is a pure creator, and he presides over a world that wants to reinvent itself. Nostalgia for a lost Garden of Eden has come to an end, as humans feel strong enough to shape a world that will express their own creative urges. This is a stage of new power. It contains so much energy and vitality that detachment can be put to good use as a shield from outside distractions.

The tangled hierarchy in stage five is dominated by the following:

creativity
art and science
exploration
rebelliousness
insistence on freedom
focus

bursts of inspiration

unbounded energy

intolerance for limits

anti-authority

All these words apply to the great forerunners of human history, from Galileo to Einstein. They are the explorers of consciousness, with no tolerance for being confined. The God of this stage resembles them but on an infinite scale. Instead of creating the world and sitting back in absentia, God is constantly creating; genesis is an eternal process that takes place in infinite dimensions.

Leaders at this stage are exemplars of humanity. Time and place give way. A Newton or a Mozart inspires generations across centuries, ignoring national boundaries. True creators are so powerful that politics, with its rough and tumble of competing interests, can't contain them. Napoleon was a self-proclaimed member of this level, and he spent every waking hour remaking France in his image, from the legal system down to the buttons on the coats of his soldiers, from public monuments to tastes in food and fashion. This unsurpassed period ended when he became a monster of ego and destroyed himself. By wanting everything in the world stamped with his name, he lost the creative connection that had made him seem superhuman for two decades. (Napoleon wound up being a very ordinary man, sitting in his bathtub on Saint Helena dictating memories of forgotten glory. He himself was aware that the creative connection had been broken forever.)

The unworkable tactic in stage five is that a new world cannot be invented by any individual, however inspired. Great artists live in a fantasy of totally unhindered creativity, yet their power ends on the page and the canvas. On the other hand, inspiration is a powerful force, and for the moments when we are in the presence of a genius's great creations, we feel lifted up to a higher level of truth.

Two other problems still limit stage five: anarchy and isolation. Creators hate restraint and despise authority (one only has to read Michelangelo's endless complaints about Pope Julius—submitting even to the supreme church authority was next to impossible emotionally). But a world of unfettered creativity would be sheer anarchy. The great creators wind up living in isolation, unable to change the world but unable to blend into it, either. God at this stage is such a pure creator that he is almost beyond human comprehension. He cannot transform humanity in his image while still allowing human frailty to exist.

Stage 6: Vision, Compassion, Love

THE GOD OF this stage loves every aspect of humanity, and he presides over a world that surrenders to him even when it isn't asked to surrender. Power turns on its head. No longer anchored in threats of any kind, it proceeds from love, asking nothing yet inspiring complete devotion. A person in this stage has become a visionary. He no longer cares about himself as an individual. Every thought and action is an expression of love for humanity itself. The labels of good and evil are almost dissolved. Every living creature is accepted in the embrace of compassion.

In stage six the tangled hierarchy is dominated by the following:

vision
compassion
miracles
complete transformation

end of personality
future-oriented
ego death
surrender

The God of stage six is barely attached to time and space. He inspires visionaries who live for the transformation that will one day bring heaven on earth. Instead of being interested in everyday events, visionaries have the faculty of second attention: they can see the approach of a transformed humanity. Buddha and Jesus, Socrates and Lao-Tze, Mohammed and Confucius stand on the threshold between time and the timeless. They translate eternal existence into human possibility.

This threshold is a magical place because here the iron laws of matter and energy are softened. Visionaries can perform miracles. They alter reality itself. In that sense they are like meta-creators. Without using physical materials, their influence causes the future to change through invisible means. I love a phrase I heard years ago: *These are the people who precipitate reality on to the Earth.*

God at this stage is pure blessing, pure grace. His light answers prayers by infusing gross reality with a divine presence. This can be felt in the very holiest places. There are always spiritual communities at those places, since the people who can sense this fragrance of divinity want to be around it as much as they can. At this stage the revered teachers of mankind become saints, pure vehicles for God's grace.

Life in stage six contains no duality. The problem of judgment has disappeared. Nobody is seen as evil or unacceptable. No event is outside God's intent. The worst aspects of human life are blessed so that they can be transformed. There is a vestige of struggle left in the war for human souls, but that is just a symbol that comes from a lower perspective. The light doesn't go to war.

It pervades all of creation and waits with infinite patience to be noticed. There is one stage of evolution ahead, because the domain of eternity still beckons. That domain is beyond change or transformation, and it acknowledges no distinction between past, present, and future.

Stage 7: Unity, Being, Eternity

IN THIS, THE final stage of evolution, God loses all qualities. He is no longer here or there, in or out, near or far. He has become pure being. His only attribute is expressed in the voice from the burning bush, which said to Moses, *I am that I am.* The world such a God presides over is completely unified. All differences have melted away. Evolution is no more. The seeker has arrived, not at the end or the beginning, but at the source.

In stage seven the tangled hierarchy has also disappeared. This final state is beyond words and is best described by what it isn't:

uncreated
undying
boundless
timeless
beyond opposites
beyond thought
inconceivable

This leaves one supreme adjective. Stage seven is *real.* A person who has come this far has been stripped of all illusions. He experiences only what is eternally true. I cannot pretend to give a picture of this state in terms of how it must feel. I am not even sure who has dwelled in it, given that the most ancient spiritual documents, such as the *Rig Veda,* have no author. The sources of such primordial documents have been given names like Vyassa and Vashistha, but their actual identities have been swept away in the tide of history.

The state of unity is not mythical, however. It lies at the core of every spiritual tradition. It is spoken of whenever a great teacher is pushed to answer the question, *Who am I?* Six different answers can be given to that question, one to fit each major stage of consciousness. But eventually curiosity, tinged with wonder, wants to know the *real* answer, which is "You are That," the uncreated pure essence from which all creation flows. "That" is the molding clay which God uses to create anything. Before there is light or darkness there is That; before there is good and evil there is That. Duality springs from it like a statue springing from raw clay; duality is swallowed up again like a statue melted back into raw clay.

With this complete picture of the evolution of consciousness at hand, we can define exactly what war is and how God relates to it.

MAKING SENSE OF GOD AND WAR

Stage 1. War is struggle born of fear. God encourages the struggle and takes sides.

Stage 2. War is competition for lands, money, and power. God is on the side of the winner.

Stage 3. War is a struggle to get peace. God is the champion of peace.

Stage 4. War is the work to make harmony out of differences. God includes everything in harmony.

Stage 5. War is the inspired effort to reach beyond limitation to create a new world. God is the progenitor of all new worlds.

Stage 6. War is the last vestige of good versus evil. God is a vision of heaven regained.

Stage 7. War is nonexistent. God lives in every moment of being.

This list tells us that in the tangled hierarchy, nobody was wrong in his or her view of God, but nobody was completely right, either. We are all living within the seven stages of consciousness. When one attracts us and dominates our minds, it doesn't block our sense of the others. The sufferer clouded by fear can also experience moments of being embraced by the highest state of unity. At the level of the soul we all know this about ourselves. With the broadest view, we can have patience with the many faces of war and the many faces of God. The important thing is the eternal journey of transformation. On that road no one is ever at war with anyone else.

THE METAPHYSICS
OF TERROR

ANOTHER BEHEADING OCCURRED today. An American civilian named Eugene Armstrong, a middle-aged man with thinning hair and a trimmed graying beard, sat rocking on the floor, blindfolded, as his masked tormentors talked into the camera. The habit of videoing these beheadings for display on the Internet now seems ritualized. Armstrong was kidnapped from his home in central Baghdad last week, one of two Americans and a Briton to fall into the hands of a jihadist group. This time the group is demanding the release of Iraqi women being held in American-run jails. The U.S. Army says that there are no such women, only two civilians detained elsewhere for suspected work in Saddam Hussein's biological weapons program. No one has said whether these two women, nicknamed Doctor Germ and Mrs. Anthrax by the Americans, will be released. If not, the terrorists promise to execute the other two hostages tomorrow.

The room in which Armstrong sat was papered with photos of detainees being held in the prison camps at Guantanamo Bay in Cuba. The masked men's message to the camera goes on and on, a rambling diatribe against America. When the deed is done, it is too gruesome to contemplate. With utmost barbarity Armstrong was decapitated with a knife and his body thrown out into the streets to be retrieved and identified.

I am painting the scene with no sadistic intent—I did not see the video myself—but only to place you as near as I can to the black horror that such acts of terror create. And are meant to create. President Bush vowed that the terrorists would not break America's will, as he did when this string of beheadings began two years ago in Pakistan, where the American journalist Daniel Pearl was killed. Bush branded the terrorists ideologues of hatred. Like every ideology, terror is based on its own belief system. The tenets of that belief system strike peaceful people as unbelievably cruel:

Murder is a viable political tool.

Terror is the only means to wake up the conscience of the world to massive injustice.

Targeting civilians is crucial, because their deaths create maximum terror.

Terror is the only thing governments will listen to.

In the chaos created by terror, oppressed people can seize power and force an end to their suffering.

Explaining the belief system of Al-Qaida and the other terrorist groups is problematic, for in a way it does them too much credit to call these tenets the result of considered thought. Terrorism operates outside of morality; it has no law or rules. It disobeys every instinct of tolerance and uses intellect to justify something that cannot be justified. The rules being violated are ones that hold civil society together:

Murder is a crime, and murder of innocents the ultimate crime.

Chaos is the enemy of happiness; it achieves nothing.

Barbarity is intolerable to an orderly society living under the rule of law.

Trying to end suffering by creating a different kind of suffering is deeply immoral.

To protect these rules America has become the avowed enemy of terrorism. To many people, questioning this commitment is itself immoral. But each of us must confront this new ideology of the jihadists and their kind, because every sign points to stateless terror being the greatest threat in the new century. The way of peace cannot ignore the existence of extremism and its inhuman cruelty as a political force. The power of love must find a way to overcome its opposite, whether you label that opposite hatred, evil, or fear.

I think the conflict between terrorism and love is the crucial one that faces us now. For many, this statement in itself will seem like an admission of defeat. Love is tender, soft, vulnerable, feminine, yielding, forgiving, and nonviolent. Terrorism is hard, unforgiving, brutal, masculine, aggressive, and intolerant. (I am using masculine and feminine to describe an ethos, realizing that of course men can love and women can commit terrorist acts.) On physical grounds, terrorism would appear to be so strong that opposing it with equal violence, intolerance, and unforgiving resolve is the only sane choice. Can love stop a suicide bomber? Can love prevent a beheading? If the answer is no, then love cannot be the answer to a jihadist determined to die while taking as many civilian casualties along as possible.

Yet the way of peace tells us that the physical evidence is misleading. Power can be found at deeper levels than the physical. The ideology of the jihadist is rootless and desperate. It cannot seize the real power on the planet, which comes from people's hopes and aspirations. Love is on the right side; it is supported by the soul and by the expansion of consciousness everywhere.

Standing up to terrorists is basically a police action. Yet the police are only effective if a criminal would rather give up than die. The classic police ultimatum—*Come out with your hands up or we'll shoot*—is useless against someone who is motivated by dying. In this way the tactics of terrorism have entered a new phase, similar to the kamikaze flyers over the Pacific in World War II, where ordinary rules don't apply and ordinary solutions won't work.

There is a spiritual saying which holds that the darkness rises to meet the light, meaning that every step foward that consciousness takes attracts its opposite. We don't get the enemies we deserve. We get the enemies that are forced to show themselves when the light shines brighter, like vermin scurrying out from under a rock when it's overturned. Before the rock was turned over they were out of sight, but once exposed, they can be dealt with. The analogy ends here, because the darkness terrorism has exposed won't end by exterminating it. The light is a healing light; its work is to bring every person into a more evolved state.

The power of evolution is never on the side of hatred, so if we expect to evolve past the grim specter of terrorism, we need to confront the powerful reactions that terror inspires, primarily two:

> *These people stand for evil, and probably absolute evil.*
> *The horrors they commit make me want to kill them.*

The more brutal the acts of terror, the easier it is to believe that Al-Qaida's members are bestial, so I was especially shocked to read the story of Ayman al-Zawahri, who is often called bin Laden's right-hand man, his brain trust, and the real author of almost every terror attack in the Middle East. The first surprise came from reading that Al-Zawahri is an eye surgeon. He comes from a prominent family of doctors and scholars in Cairo; his father was a professor of pharmacology before he died in 1995.

Al-Zawahri could have settled for a life of ease and privilege, but by the age of fifteen he was being arrested for illegal activities based on his fervor for fundamentalism. He had joined the Muslim Brotherhood, an old and established fundamentalist group. In the following years, all through medical school and beyond, Al-Zawahri continued to make trouble, and steadily he became more radicalized. How does a good mind warp? Oppression by the existing powers plays a part. Sympathy for a creed that the state wants to repress, and for the poor people who mostly comprise fundamentalist followers, is also a key ingredient. Poverty and politics are an explosive combination.

Through this man I can put a face on terror, although I can follow his mind only so far. Al-Zawahri may be a psychopath. He probably masterminded the 9/11 attacks. He certainly signed bin Laden's infamous *fatwah* in 1998 that called for attacks on Western tourists. One sees him in blurry videotapes taken in bin Laden's mountain retreat somewhere in Pakistan or Afghanistan vowing revenge against the United States. And yet he also served on a mercy mission as a doctor aiding the Muslim freedom fighters in their resistance to Russia in the Afghan war, at the same time that bin Laden was putting his fortune to humanitarian use in the same struggle.

There is a long tradition of brilliant minds turning to terrorism. Stalin and Trotsky controlled an entire country by that means. The founding of Israel is deeply enmeshed with the terror tactics of the Zionist underground group known as the Irgun. (Their 1946 attack on the British army forces headquartered in the King David Hotel in Jerusalem was a key event in the birth trauma of the future state of Israel.) History determines who will be vilified as a ruthless killer and who glorified as a freedom fighter. Yasser Arafat and other terrorists past and present call themselves freedom fighters, but they might well be labeled criminals in the end.

But as I look at Al-Zawahri's face, his thick scholarly spectacles framing an expression that could be read as totally determined and heartless, I know that he harbors no image of himself as evil. He is an ideologue whose analytical mind has led him to believe that when you are opposed by a superpower, when your Arab homelands are ruled by corrupt dictators and royal families, when the fabric of traditional values is about to fall apart through poverty and widespread social injustice, there is no alternative but terrorism. It becomes both medicine and addiction, an excuse to end injustice that carries you high on the thrills of rebellion.

Contrary to what we hear, the real enemy of peace isn't evil but chaos. In a state of chaos such as terrorism wants to create, society breaks down. Chaos isn't the same as evil. It affects people in ways that you can't predict. When Baghdad fell and Saddam Hussein's army disappeared overnight, the Iraqi populace looted everything in sight, not only the palaces and headquarters of the Baath party but every school and university. Mental patients were thrown out of their beds so that the beds could be stolen, along with all the medicines and supplies. In the 1996 racial riots in Los Angeles, black communities were looted and burned by their own residents. Chaos is irrational. The Iraqi looters were hurting themselves as surely as the L.A. rioters were. (In the aftermath of the riots many banks and other businesses refused to reopen.)

On a grander scale the descent of Russia into chaos after the dissolution of the Soviet Union was more startling. The Russian mafia began to flourish under capitalism, getting anything it wanted by intimidation and force. Ruthless oligarchs made billions from mining operations and utilities formerly owned by the state, siphoning their money out of the country into Swiss bank accounts. At the level of the common citizen, there was a widespread refusal to pay any form of income tax, leaving the treasury with a tax base of about ten percent of what it should have been. President Putin announced in 2002 that if the country tightened its belt and made a massive effort to recover, in a decade Russia might achieve the same standard of living as Portugal, the poorest country in NATO.

This tells us that anyone can fall prey to chaos and descend into self-destructive behavior as a result. *Evil* isn't a useful term here. Difficult as it is to believe, terrorists don't see themselves as evil. They see themselves as revolutionaries, and more than that as idealists who are willing to make enormous sacrifices in order to bring about a better world.

To Western eyes, the Taliban regime in Afghanistan was intolerably cruel and fanatic. Women suspected of adultery were routinely stoned or executed in the public soccer stadium of Kabul. Women were forbidden to hold jobs; former executives at the state radio station overnight found themselves reduced to the status of wandering beggars and prostitutes. No woman was allowed medical care, even for childbirth, or any form of education. Yet in the Arab world Afghanistan under the Taliban was held up as an Islamic paradise.

Did evil see a monstrous rebirth there? Was the thin veneer of civilization stripped away, allowing free rein to the force of barbarism? You may think either of these things, but what strikes me is that the Taliban see themselves as virtuous, even utopian, in their aims. Creating such a false sense of self is the main effect of ideology.

In the 1930s during the infamous show trials under Stalin, hundreds of educated people, including prominent artists and intellectuals, publicly confessed their sins against the true way of Communism. Despite their innocence of wildly trumped-up charges, a combination of fear and ideological brainwashing motivated these people to voluntarily walk to their own doom, for confession didn't save their lives. Now cleansed of their sin, they were sent to the Gulag or to execution. The Soviet state was an archenemy of religion, and yet it managed to duplicate the surrealism of the Spanish Inquisition, when heretics were burned at the stake but strangled first as an act of mercy if they confessed their sin. Besides chaos, then, the next greatest enemy of peace is ideology, because in its grip even civilized people argue themselves out of their humanity.

Ideology is especially treacherous because it offers the opposite of what it promises. To any balanced mind the Islamic paradise in Afghanistan was as desolate as the workers' paradise under Stalin or the Maoist paradise in China. What makes our times peculiar is that the chief opponents of Islam have arisen from a rival brand of ideology. To many fundamentalist Christians, the war of terrorism is a holy war. In 2003 a three-star general named William Boykin found himself condemned throughout the Arab world as a bigot for a speech he gave in church.

Boykin, a devout fundamentalist, feels blameless for remarks he made during a sermon he preached on the theme of a soldier's faith in God. He had been recalling his experience in the ill-fated invasion of Somalia ten years earlier in 1993, when America's expressed mission was to overthrow corrupt warlords who used violence to preside over a state of absolute chaos and famine. When a follower of one warlord defiantly told Boykin that he would be protected by Allah, Boykin's response was, "I knew that my God was bigger than his. I knew that my God was a real God, and his was an idol."

In the furor over these remarks, Boykin was painted as an

anti-Muslim zealot. He tried to backtrack by explaining that the idol he was referring to was his enemy's distorted version of Allah, not the true Allah. But I was struck by the general's view of the war in Somalia as an enterprise not of this earth. "God showed me that the enemy was not the enemy I could see. That the enemy is in the spiritual realm." As vehemently as he might resist the comparison, this is the precise attitude that pairs Christian and Islamic fundamentalism: both see the current war on terrorism as otherworldly, a battle for souls. And in such a battle there is every reason to show no mercy. As General Boykin says, "The enemy is a spiritual enemy. He is called the principality of darkness. He is a guy called Satan."

We have become used to the jihadists who refer to America as the great Satan, but hearing the same rhetoric thrown back is deeply disturbing. The beheading of an innocent American is a barbaric cruelty performed in the name of God. We feel a shudder of horror, even though we cannot find quite the same horror or tears for innocent Iraqi children ripped apart by shrapnel from American cluster bombs. If we go a step further and say that the deaths we inflict are part of God's plan, we are fated to descend into the same unreal world as the jihadist.

Our version of that hellish world is air-conditioned and provided with hundreds of cable channels, but those cosmetic differences won't save us. Last year I was invited to get acquainted with a wealthy oil man who wanted to meet me at an expensive country club. He greeted me warmly, professing to admire me and wanting me to align with the Bush team. He was part of the current innermost circle in political power, he said. We began a round of golf, and once he felt comfortable he said, "Of course, we'd need you to show us that you accept Jesus Christ as your personal lord and savior."

I tried not to look startled and told him that I revered Christ as an enlightened soul and great teacher (which was not mere politeness from someone who went to Christian-run schools as a child in India and has been deeply influenced by reading the New Testament). But my answer wasn't good enough. He waited a few moments, as we each hit our ball to the green, then he said, "But you have to see the big picture. These Muslims are evil, and we have to wipe out every single one of them."

The undercurrent of ideology is particularly disturbing because fanaticism has learned to wear a business suit and hire smooth speech writers. However, the underlying intolerance is just as bald. Like General Boykin, the oil man would ferociously defend himself against the charge of fanaticism. Boykin, in his own mind, was speaking a simple, heartfelt truth when he gave his opinion of how the rancorous 2000 presidential election turned out. "Why is this man [Bush] in the White House? The majority of Americans did not vote for him. He's in the White House because God put him there for a time such as this."

So what exactly is this time?

To the jihadist it is a time when the true faith must be saved from the threat of the infidel. The corrupt West has defiled and betrayed the tenets of Islam. It has stolen Islam's holiest places and supported Israel in its intolerable possession of Jerusalem. Modernism spreads its secular influence, smothering the commands of God. If those commands continue to be disobeyed, innocent Muslims will find themselves in hell. God knows this and has armed his true sons and daughters so that they may win Paradise through martyrdom.

To the fervent evangelical Christian it is the End Time, the preceding turmoil that signals a great apocalyptic drama. The stakes are cosmic, because we will soon see the rise of the Anti-Christ in the Middle East. Mortal combat will follow, guided from behind the scenes by Satan and Christ. Thousands are destined to die, but at the Last Judgment God will find his own, who will be resurrected in their bodies to join Christ in heaven.

This is fantastic, other-worldly belief. Fantastic, that is, unless your consciousness has been shaped by it.

Many explanations have been put forth for why apocalyptic thinking has proved so seductive right now. Modernism is blamed for pushing ordinary people beyond their comfort zones. When the mass media assaults us with a flood of violent images, threat goes into overload. We long to escape into a world apart, as promised by God. We long, too, for redemption, a force as old as religion. Details of ordinary life alarm the fundamentalists. Chaos on the highway every day in traffic jams. Americans moving restlessly from town to town rather than becoming rooted in a community. On the global level this translates into the unprecedented number of refugees and homeless in the world. We face overpopulation and the insufferable crowding of polluted cities. There is economic uncertainty, too, the sudden surplus of discontented, unemployed young males in the Middle East (some Arab countries have a majority of the population under the age of eighteen), and much else besides: old religious grudges flaring up once more, the spread of evangelism, and more subtly the quiet flight of many educated middle-class people away from the faiths they were brought up in.

Looking at these one by one, no reason quite hits the mark, however. They sound like items in a think-tank report or a university department of sociology. Yet *something* has happened. I feel it, and I'm sure you do, too. Whatever the causes may be, we are all enmeshed in this shift. Only by realizing that fact can we escape the automatic reflex that makes us think, *"These people are evil"* and *"They make me want to kill them."* Empathy is its own reward. If you can see yourself in the same context as those who threaten you, you will open a way for reason, and the steady decrease of fear.

Extremism has human roots. In 1961 Israel put on trial "the man in the glass booth," the notorious Nazi Adolf Eichmann. The Nuremberg trials of the postwar era were long over, but some prominent Nazis had escaped capture. Eichmann was among the most important. He was tracked down to Argentina and kidnapped by Israeli intelligence as part of a campaign to bring every person who had committed crimes against humanity to justice.

There was no doubt that Eichmann's crimes were monstrous, but the man himself was drab and ordinary. He occasioned the phrase *the banality of evil,* which doesn't mean that Eichmann's actions were banal but that evil deeds grow out of everyday circumstances. In this case the world was faced with the mystery of how a traveling salesman who had lost his job was transformed into a lieutenant colonel in the S.S. and put in charge, as chief of the Gestapo's Jewish department, of Hitler's mass exterminations.

Since the same mystery faces us with the rise of terrorism, I'd like to explore the details of Eichmann's story. He was born into a middle-class German family but suffered the misfortune of faring worse than his father. His father owned a small mining company, but Adolf wound up being a common laborer. For a time he worked in the family business, then he left home to become a traveling salesman of electrical supplies. He was in his late twenties when he jointed the Austrian Nazi Party in 1932, one of innumerable young men disaffected by the First World War and thrown into economic chaos by the Depression. Such men were eager to find a scapegoat for their sense of powerlessness and rage; Hitler provided the perfect means.

Having lost his sales job, Eichmann received a year's military training under the Nazis in 1933-34, but he came into his own as a bureaucrat. He had a talent for paperwork and organization, skills that even a terror regime values. He was assigned to Heinrich Himmler's security department and became an expert on Jewish questions. Eichmann went so far as to learn a smattering of Hebrew and Yiddish; in 1937 he visited Palestine—at that point the Nazis were considering the possibility of deporting the Jews to their own Zionist homeland. (Abraham Lincoln similarly flirted with the idea of returning slaves back to Africa, although in both cases history took a more violent turn.)

At first Eichmann was a mere functionary who controlled the permits Jews needed if they wanted to leave Austria and Czechoslovakia. Then the noose tightened, and he became the official who oversaw "forced emigration," the policy that threw 150,000 Jews who did not want to emigrate out of their homes. As the Final Solution began to be implemented, this policy turned into forced evacuation, and Eichmann's bureaucratic skills blossomed into the full-blown evil of rounding up, processing, and transporting millions of Jews to the concentration camps. The period of time it took Eichmann to rise was short; by 1939, four years after his assignment under Himmler, he was a full-fledged mass murderer. He personally helped develop the gassing techniques that made genocide efficient, and witnesses recall scenes where he sat at the window peering into the gas chambers to satisfy himself that death was being administered as quickly as possible to the maximum number of victims.

That this involved watching screaming women and children piling onto each other in a desperate effort to escape the gas didn't touch Eichmann, although no doubt their faces came very close to his on the other side of the window. Like terrorists today, Eichmann was shielded by ideology. To him, this really was a solution to grievous social ills. The Reich was holy in its mission to purify the race. He could never accept the label of monster that the rest of the world attached to him (the trial records of all the Nazi war criminals reveal almost no admissions of guilt and remorse). Eichmann went so far as to declare that he personally was no anti-Semite; his zeal was for efficiency and organization. He never complained about the hardships of his workers in the death camps or himself. Chiefly he complained that the monthly quota of human shipments was not being met.

Eichmann's facelessness saved his life for a while. Not having been pointed out when he was captured at the end of the war, he managed to escape an American detainee camp in 1946. He lived the next fourteen years under an assumed identity until Israeli secret agents tracked him down in a suburb outside Buenos Aires. His trial in the late spring and summer of 1961 was followed by the sentence of death, which was carried out by hanging on June 1, 1962. Eichmann's body was cremated and his ashes scattered at sea in international waters.

This one man's life exemplifies many of the forces we've talked about: economic and social chaos disrupted his life. An ideology attracted his allegiance and blinded him to reality. He fell under the sway of otherworldly apocalyptic thinking that promised a utopia through violence. Other potent factors also contributed (and are prevalent today), such as the rise of a charismatic leader, hatred of a common enemy, the appeal to racial unity, and the humiliation of masculine pride. And yet explaining how an ordinary person becomes a monster isn't that simple. Or is it? Forty years ago a famous experiment was conducted at Yale by psychologist Stanley Millgram. Volunteers entered a room and were told that they were taking part in an experiment that would determine how punishment affected learning. Each was matched to a subject who had been connected to wires that could administer an electric shock. This subject was called "the student" whose ability to learn would be tested. The procedure was to ask a series of questions, and for every question the student got wrong, the volunteer (or teacher) would press a button to send a shock. Every wrong question brought a stronger shock. Clearly marked on the dial in front of the teacher were the voltages being administered, up to 450, or twice the amount that runs through household current. After that the dial read XXX.

How hard do you think it would be to get you to send 450 volts of electricity into someone's body? Millgram picked his subjects from the Yale community and the surrounding town, yet sixty-five percent were willing to give the maximum shock. They weren't comfortable doing it. Their victims, the students, screamed with pain and even resorted to shouting for mercy, followed by moaning, and finally slumping over, unconscious. Yet even then the white-coated technician who was in the room to monitor the experiment told the subjects that no answer counted as a wrong answer, requiring them to administer a stronger shock.

As it happened, there were no shocks and the students were actors. Millgram wasn't actually testing the relationship of pain and learning. He was testing how susceptible ordinary people are to authority. His findings were disturbing, yet future experiments validated his conclusions that the line between a normal person and a monster is thinner than we imagine.

A 1971 experiment at Stanford University set up a fake prison with certain students acting the part of guards and others the part of prisoners. The guards were given free rein to treat the prisoners any way they wished, but the experiment had to be stopped after a week because the guards' behavior exceeded the most outrageous expectations. In a haunting foreshadowing of the events in Iraq at the Abu Ghraib prison, the guards humiliated their charges, stripped them naked, put hoods over their heads, and goaded them into sexual acts. This despite the fact that there was no ethnic hostility or class difference at work, no heightened animosity due to war. The psychologist who conducted the Stanford prison experiment was asked his opinion of the Abu Ghraib torture by U.S. personnel and said, "It's not that we put bad apples in a good barrel. We put good apples in a bad barrel. The barrel corrupts anything that it touches." Consciousness is undoubtedly malleable. It can be made to conform to unreality, untruth, and to every variety of inhumane conditions.

There is still cause for hope, however, because the forces that turn a person into a terrorist are not mundane. If you want someone to cross the line from normal to monster, you must supply the following conditions:

Give him permission to disregard morality.
Put an authority close by to reinforce the cruelty, making it a duty.
Arrange a hierarchy so that lower ranks must obey upper ranks.
Create an atmosphere of fear.
Apply group pressure by showing that everyone else is going along.
Release the evil deed from any threat of being punished.
Do everything behind closed doors.

These are specific conditions that can be reversed before great evil arises. They applied to the Spanish Inquisition, to the Salem witch trials, and to the Nazi concentration camps. Those horrors are the exception because if you remove the atmosphere of fear or install an authority who forbids cruelty, torture isn't able to flourish. In Millgram's experiment it was found that minor changes were extremely powerful. If the white-coated authority figure wasn't in the room to give orders, the subjects were no longer willing to shock the students to any level near the maximum. If the person being shocked wasn't placed behind glass but took a position across the table from the one administering the shock, this closeness made most people stop what they were doing very quickly.

By contrast, the metaphysics of love doesn't need special circumstances backed up by authority figures. In the absence of a distorting ideology, the natural course of everyone's awareness is attracted to love. Love is stronger than terror because ultimately every impulse can be traced back to our deep need for love. Your awareness knows this; it knows it even when the cloak of turmoil covers over the truth. The conditions that turn consciousness toward love are simple.

Giving love to others and receiving it back.
Sitting alone in your own silence.
Immersing yourself in natural beauty.
Making art and appreciating art in all its forms.
Telling the truth, whatever the consequences.
Laughing, dancing, playing with a child.
Having any outlet for joy.
Communing with deep emotions.
Acting out of kindness and compassion.
Bonding, feeling at one with a group whose goals are positive.
Offering yourself in service.

The texture of everyday life is far removed from the conditions that create terrorism, and as Muslim fundamentalists begin to value these things and to experience them in place of their widespread agitation, the force of love will work patiently but irresistibly to create change. I cannot say whether this will happen in our lifetime, but it's certain that we are all attracted to feeling safe, worthy, at peace with ourselves, sexually gratified, and loved. These are basic needs, and the truth is that even under horrendous conditions, people try to hold onto them.

One of the greatest stories of courage through love comes from Nadezhda Mandelstam, the widow of one of Russia's greatest modern poets. Her husband, Osip Mandelstam, was born in 1891, and was therefore a young man at the time of the Russian Revolution. He was immune to the pressures of the Soviet system, however, and pursued his own course. His work did not fall into the accepted realistic style demanded under Stalin, which cost him his livelihood, but Mandelstam went on to mourn the direction of Russian society as it declined into terror and oppression.

For this he was deported from Moscow in 1934, only to return and be rearrested in 1938. This time Stalin ordered him to a labor camp, and apparently he died along the way. His wife recalls that when she was given the news of her husband's death, it was on the very day that Soviet writers, for the first time, were being given prizes by the state. The news of Mandelstam's death arrived during a party of younger writers celebrating their awards. As she recounts:

> Fadeyev shed a drunken tear for M. "We have done away with a great poet!" The celebration took on something of the flavor of a surreptitious wake for the dead. I am not clear, however, as to who there . . . really understood what M.'s destruction meant. Most of them, after all, belonged to the generation which had changed its values in favor of the "new." It was they who had prepared the way for the strong man, the dictator who was empowered to kill or spare people at his own discretion, to establish goals and choose whatever means he saw fit for their fulfillment.

Nadezhda Mandelstam was determined that her husband's poetry would survive. Everything he wrote was banned and out of print. It was a crime to be caught with banned literature, so she hid all the manuscripts that she could lay her hands on. She spent months memorizing hundreds of verses and then she waited.

For twenty years she kept silent. The government watched her constantly. She was given minor teaching posts with a pittance for a salary, and she knew that some of her best students, the ones who came up and eagerly asked her to recite one of Osip Mandel-stam's poems, were spies, planted in her class by the KGB. Her only safety lay in pretending that his work no longer existed, which was exactly the fate dictated for it by the state.

Twenty years later, there was a thaw in the Cold War. Stalin was denounced in the Central Committee, and at last Nadezhda Mandelstam could begin to release the lost poems. It is thanks to her efforts that we have most of what survives of a great artist. Her 1970 memoir, *Hope Against Hope,* is one of the most touching in modern literature, a classic of the persistence of love. The shadow of Stalinism continues to darken Russia as the central govern-ment pursues its brutal tactics against Chechnya, yet one woman acting out of love gave us something that will endure much longer than terrorism or ideology. Here is a sample of Osip Mandel-stam's delicate, dreamlike work. Even in translation I hear a voice that speaks beyond time and death.

A FLAME IS IN MY BLOOD

A flame is in my blood, burning dry life, to the bone.
I do not sing of stone, now, I sing of wood.
It is light and coarse: made of a single spar,
the oak's deep heart, and the fisherman's oar.
Drive them deep, the piles: hammer them in tight,
around wooden Paradise, where everything is light.

THE BODY AT PEACE

Conflict resolution has become a major topic for scholars, university courses, and Ph.D. theses, yet I doubt this has advanced the cause of peace very much. When I remarked to a diplomatic group that we would never end terrorism until we endeared ourselves to the enemy, they stared at me as if I had lost my mind. I get much the same reaction whenever I say that the safest country would be one with no army and no weapons. (The Vatican is such a state, as are places like Monaco, Luxembourg, many Caribbean and Pacific islands, and Costa Rica, but we dismiss them as either special cases or as too insignificant to count.) Conflicts aren't resolved when two parties walk away with residual animosity.

The way of peace needs to replace the current style of negotiation, which has obviously proved futile. I was in the audience when a spiritual teacher was asked about the Middle East and whether diplomacy would ever succeed there. "How can it?" he replied. "Diplomacy is just lying gracefully."

As a remark it had the ring of truth. When two warring nations get together to talk peace, their diplomats have to lie about what is actually going on. What is actually going on is irrational, confused, brutal, and full of anger, because that is the nature of war. The newspapers in both countries will be full of accusations about innocent civilians being targeted on purpose. There will be charges of war crimes and atrocities by the other side. The mood on the street will be rancorous, and the brazen rhetoric of God and country will be in full flight.

With a sinking heart one looks at a string of declared diplomatic triumphs that were nothing like that in reality. The classic example is a famous 1993 photograph taken on the White House lawn. On one side the PLO leader Yasser Arafat, wearing his customary Arab headdress and brown army uniform, has extended his hand to the Israeli prime minister, Yitzhak Rabin, who is dressed in a dark business suit. The sun shines brightly over them, although not as brightly as the smile worn by President Clinton, his arms outstretched in an open embrace that draws the two arch enemies together.

What triumph were they celebrating? The fact that these two opponents had never shaken hands before in public. Behind the scenes they could barely tolerate each other, and the formal Declaration of Principles that they were signing that day was a sham. Soon Rabin would be assassinated by one of his own citizens, while Arafat would continue the perilous zigzag of terror and negotiations that has brought endless suffering to the Palestinian people. More than a decade later there is not a shred of the old accords left, and who has to be told that the two sides are locked in a bloodier conflict than ever?

We cannot pretend to be friends across the table and remain enemies in our hearts. The famous adage that war is an extension of diplomacy only makes sense when we admit that the opposite is also true: diplomacy is an extension of war. Graceful lying is a front for a campaign of death that only eases up when neither side can kill enough of the other side to declare total victory.

Before Rabin and Arafat there was Henry Kissinger sitting across the table from the North Vietnamese in Paris. Both he and Le Duc Tho would win the Nobel Peace Prize in 1973 for ending the Vietnam War, yet I doubt that they mentioned what was actually going on for even a moment, emotionally speaking. If they had, the American position might have sounded like this: *I am powerful and strong. I could wipe you out with one blow to get what I want, but something is holding me back, so I'm giving you a chance to survive. Take my offer before I really get mad and crush you.* The North Vietnamese position might have sounded like this: *You can't hurt me enough to win. You've attacked my home and family, and I'd rather die than see you in my home. You think I'm weaker than you, but I've found out how to hurt you anyway, and hurt you badly.* These are the feelings that must be confronted by the way of peace. Peace has powerful means to bring people out of their distorted sense that violence is their only choice.

PEACEFUL RESOLUTIONS

How to negotiate conflicts through peace

Show respect for your opponent

Recognize perceived injustice

Believe in forgiveness

Bond at the emotional level

Desist in belligerent actions

Recognize values that are opposed to yours

Don't pass judgment and make your opponent wrong

Don't talk in terms of ideology

Confront the underlying factor of fear

As sophisticated as modern war has become, nations seem to overlook these extremely simple and human dictums. Why do we need to be told to respect our enemies? Because we feel insulted when they don't respect us. No one can negotiate with an opponent who is disdainful and contemptuous. In the dialogue with the Arab world, the West's attitude has been thinly veiled contempt, and so it is no wonder that so little progress has been made. Let me support each item on the list with arguments that go beyond the posturing of war.

Show respect for your opponent. The mistake here is to replace respect with force. The warrior's argument is always that a country wins respect by pummeling the enemy and beating respect into him. In our current climate, this argument is being advanced as the only way to deal with the Arab mentality. Israel adopted this position when it vowed to kill one (or more) Palestinians for every Israeli lost in terror attacks. The U.S. and other allies applauded, and yet the result is obvious today as the occupied territories rage with violence from which there seems to be no escape. Yet Arabs and Israelis live within blocks of each other in Jerusalem; Palestinians crossing the border to their jobs in Israel are a key factor in the economies of both sides. In many ways they cannot do without each other. But there is no fundamental respect between them.

To an outsider who belongs to neither religion, the claims regarding Jerusalem as a holy city look equal. Respect belongs to both faiths. I have been told time and again by professional negotiators that apparently insurmountable obstacles melt away once each opponent really believes that his side is being treated equally. This is a basic tenet in the way of peace, but until warring parties act on it, disputes of the kind that rage in the Middle East will continue.

Recognize perceived injustice. The mistake here is to believe that only you have been injured. Every dispute revolves around that perception. Both parties always perceive that they are owed something. If you feel that injustice has been done to you, however, you must concede the same feelings on the other side. At the end of World War II, as a way to bring Germany to its knees, the Allies fire-bombed the beautiful medieval city of Dresden, one of the centerpieces of German culture. Every scrap of the old city, including the famous cathedral and opera house, was reduced to rubble.

The effect on demoralizing the Germans was nil. War production actually increased. In the perception of the Germans, and of history in general, the Allies committed a war crime. In their own minds, the bombing forces argued that destroying Dresden was a trifle compared to Hitler's atrocities, and yet the perceived injustice was real. The way of peace cannot proceed until each side acknowledges what it has done.

Believe in forgiveness. When it is genuine, forgiveness has tremendous power to heal. Nothing that the mind can offer—excuses, a promise of repayment, justifications of right and wrong—is a substitute for feeling that you can forgive someone who hurt you. I am still amazed at the unspoken forgiveness that a defeated Japan has shown to the U.S. since World War II. In addition to the two atom bombs dropped at Hiroshima and Nagasaki, hundreds of thousands of Japanese citizens were killed in the horrific fire-bombings that rained down, not just on Tokyo, but on every major city. As much as half the population of each city died, since the typical Japanese house of wood and paper is totally vulnerable to fire. If we lost half the population of Chicago, Detroit, San Francisco, and all our other urban areas to civilian bombing, would we be so ready to forgive?

Since 9/11, I think Americans have been waiting in silent fury to hear an apology from the Arab world, one which they deserve. But the Arab world is waiting in their own silent fury for an apology from the West, for the humiliating era of colonialism and the wanton disregard of Arab pride after World War I, when the Allies autocratically dismantled the Ottoman Empire. The truth is, they deserve an apology as well. The simple human act of giving one hasn't occurred to either side. The way of peace says that it must.

Bond at the emotional level. It can be frustrating to realize that wars begin because people don't like each other. Sometimes this comes down to only two individuals. In the 1960s the Vienna peace talks between the U.S. and the Soviet Union collapsed because President John F. Kennedy and Soviet premier Nikita Khrushchev became personal antagonists.

Emotions are directly linked to a subverbal part of the old brain. When we *feel* that we can trust someone, that counts much more than if we merely *think* we can. The emotional alignment between President Ronald Reagan and Britain's prime minister Margaret Thatcher is widely credited with the resolve that both countries showed to bring about the collapse of communism. On the other hand, no Israeli leader was ever emotionally comfortable with Yasser Arafat. The world mourned the 1981 assassination of Anwar Sadat in Egypt, because he was the first Arab leader to form a genuine emotional bond with the opposition. This was seen as his greatest crime in the eyes of the fundamentalists who killed him, however. The way of peace tells us that emotional bonding—the feeling that trust and friendship are possible—must be present.

Desist in belligerent actions. In conventional negotiations a country only wins when it holds a position of strength. Therefore it is normal to keep pounding the enemy even as you talk across the peace table. Kissinger began negotiating with the North Vietnamese secretly in a Paris apartment in 1969, while the U.S. kept up its intense assaults. These initial talks failed, and the American position persisted that only the constant application of war would lead to peace. Tens of thousands of additional lives were lost in this belief, and the end result was not victory or even the stated political end of saving South Vietnam.

The main reason we still believe that fighting brings the other side to the peace table is that wars almost always end with one side being crushed. Real peace talks would be those that began with the cessation of attack. In the Iraqi conflict after Saddam's fall America believed that without steady pressure on the insurgents there could be no hope for negotiations, while every day of the struggle brought new terrorists and jihadists streaming into the country. But if we had stopped all fighting, wouldn't the other side realize that we could resume at any moment? The threat of renewed war wouldn't be off the table. No gesture speaks more sincerely to the desire for peace than if one side ends belligerent action.

Recognize values that are opposed to yours. Conventional wisdom has it that when two parties negotiate, they try to find common ground and reasons to compromise. In reality this rarely works. In a bitter divorce if you get the house I loved and I get the art you loved, the outcome is a compromise, but it isn't peaceful. After World War I the victorious Allies split up many parts of the world, including the Middle East, the Balkans, Poland, the Baltic states, and the Rhineland, into parcels that were meant to satisfy various interests and demands. As a result, resentments grew worse; ethnic and national rivalries simmered, rising later to a boil. Within twenty years world war returned, and even today we are paying the price, as the strife in the Balkans and the Arab world bears witness.

Negotiations must begin with a recognition that your opponent has values very different from yours. If it had been originally recognized, for example, that Iraq was three separate regions dominated by Sunnis, Shiites, and Kurds, each with valid rights and traditions, no one would have drawn an arbitrary circle and said, *Those are your borders. Now you are one people. Live with it.* They couldn't live with it, not without a brutal dictator, and never have. Forced compromise is futile.

In the first-rate documentary *The Fog of War,* former secretary of defense Robert S. McNamara relives his role in the Vietnam War. He recalls the turbulence of that time and his own conflicted feelings, which he kept private even as he was being vilified publicly for waging "McNamara's war." The old man looks into the camera and says, "If only we had known the enemy." With hindsight he realized that the U.S. had almost no knowledge of the beliefs and grievances of the North Vietnamese, knew little about why they were fighting or how much resolve they actually had. This ignorance played a huge part in the war's folly and its tragic outcome. The way of peace tells us that we have to know the values of our opponents, because otherwise we will never know what is negotiable and what isn't.

Don't pass judgment and make your opponent wrong. Most wars are started because both sides think they are in the right. There is no middle ground even when one side is morally compromised in its beliefs.

The classic lesson here comes from the Civil War, a conflict that began despite the fact that Southerners knew, in their heart of hearts, that slavery was wrong. Christian morality and the sight of everyday suffering had made them keenly aware that they were committing a sin. But the North's abolitionist zeal alienated even moderate Southerners. The weight of judgment against them didn't cause beneficial change. Instead it forced a defensive posture and a refusal to negotiate. The way of peace tells us that we cannot hope to end any conflict as long as one side forces the other into defending its values.

Don't talk in terms of ideology. This is such a crucial subject that I've already devoted a whole chapter to it. Enough to say here already that wars grow much worse when they turn into a battle of belief systems. Belief systems are much more visceral than the term implies. Beliefs aren't elective. You don't merely pick and choose whether to have them. Rather, beliefs are the way we justify our whole way of life. The current culture war over gay marriage is an example. As a religious institution marriage has declined steadily since the 1970s. Many more couples are living together out of wedlock. Marriage has slowly shifted into a civil affair, presided over by city hall rather than a priest. The divorce rate hovers around fifty percent as the moral stigma attached to it becomes a thing of the past.

Despite these facts, when gays declared their desire to be married, there was outrage in a sizable section of the population: the sanctity of marriage was being attacked; the natural law that binds man and woman was being violated. Yet the very opposite was happening. Gays were affirming marriage at a time when much of the heterosexual population had given up on it. The very fact that homosexuality exists in every society at every period in history indicates that it is as natural as heterosexuality, although much less common.

Ideology makes mere facts irrelevant, however. Fundamentalists who cry out against gay marriage—and gay life in general— live in a world of self-justified beliefs. Their fervent hope is that reality will conform to their ideology one day, and when it doesn't, they fight back. The same attitude fueled communism for seventy years. The Soviet state began in a burst of ideological optimism and ended in a whimper as the ideal slowly turned into a lie. The way of peace is wise enough to tell us that all ideology must be removed from negotiations if they are to reach a realistic basis for going forward.

Confront the underlying factor of fear. Wars seem to be about anger but they are actually about fear. This is a hard fact for combatants to face. In the name of toughness and invulnerability, warring countries never admit how afraid they are of each other. It would help if they did, because mutual fear can be addressed. You only have to stop doing what frightens the other side. In the thirteenth century English archers developed the practice of arming their arrows with metal tips called bodkins. This new advance allowed them to pierce chain mail at a hundred yards. They also learned to fire longbows very rapidly, at a rate of ten to twenty arrows per minute, as opposed to using a crossbow, whose mechanism had to be slowly cranked before an arrow could be launched.

Imagine the terror that resulted when the French, who were still abiding by the chivalric code of knighthood, found that their enemy had changed the rules. No more clumsy approach on horseback by knights weighed down in suits of armor. Suddenly a band of foot soldiers pouring down a hail of arrows brought the old ways of war to an end. This escalated the cost of war, since the French had no choice but to retaliate in kind.

Why didn't both sides agree that an increase in fear was unacceptable? Weapons kept growing more unspeakable by the decade. Wasn't a gun unspeakable enough? We didn't have to proceed with the Gatling gun of the Civil War, the armored tank of the First World War, and the atom bomb. Both sides have known forever that fear can be ratcheted up. Somehow we ignore that knowledge. The way of peace brings it to the forefront. To live in fear has no justification. As Freud succinctly put it, anxiety is the most unwelcome emotion. By facing the factor of fear, nations could return to the real reason for life itself, which is to pursue happiness and spiritual truth. If promoting fear became inexcusable, wars would dissolve. All of them are in the service of fear, whatever ideology or morality might say to the contrary.

If the way of peace offers such clear solutions to conflict, why have we moved in the opposite direction for so long? Are we so hard-wired to be violent that we can't help ourselves? Some scientists believe our brains permanently contain the capacity for aggression, and when war breaks out we are simply enacting the blueprint inside us. I remember first becoming aware of this argument in the 1960s when field studies of chimpanzees in the wild introduced the notion of alpha-dominant males. By now the fact that males fight for dominance throughout the animal kingdom is a cliché, but back then it was startling to read about the parallels between animal and human behavior.

The alpha-dominant male has first choice of females for mating, fighting any other male who tries to approach. Chimps, gorillas, and baboons are promiscuous, and when the females are in heat, every male is attracted to them. The dominant male finds himself in a state of constant alert, and he winds up fighting a lot of skirmishes every day, if not every hour. To remain an alpha he has to be physically large and strong, in temperament aggressive and tirelessly competitive.

Immediately the parallel between a pack of chimps and a street gang seems obvious. The habit of physical confrontation between males, going back millions of years, explains the prevalence of aggression in every culture. At the very least, no red-blooded human male wants to be left out of the fight for success. If dominance in nature demands selfish, ruthless, unswerving competitors, then why not accept that model for ourselves, particularly if our brains are wired that way? Isn't peace a biological fantasy, a perversion of nature?

There is also the related issue of territory, which backs up this argument. Although it may look to us as though animals wander randomly in the wild, they are actually very attuned to the boundaries of their own territory. These boundaries separate tribes of baboons, prides of lions, even families of sparrows. Males once again are generally responsible for protecting these boundaries, which they do by driving off competing males who venture in to try and mate with females. The loveliness of a bird-song in the morning is beside the point to an ethologist. The air isn't full of music but of warning signals sent from male to male, saying *If you hear this, you're too close to my territory. Stay out!* The human parallel seems obvious again: war is territorial. An invading nation is trying to seize new territory, which is being defended because biology demands it, as it has for eons.

But if we go deeper into the biology of war and peace, we find that it is just as innate in us to be the opposite of aggressive over sexuality and territory. Constant war is all but unknown among primitive societies. Except for one Stone Age tribe in New Guinea whose culture was based on raiding the tribe across the river every day, anthropology doesn't indicate that aborigines exist, now or ever, in the state of constant vigilance exhibited by dominant males in a pack of baboons. Animals may have no other choice, but we do. Human society learned to seek the advantages of monogamy long ago. We made incest a taboo so that sons would not compete with fathers for the sexual favors of the mother. Males learned to bond as friends. We found surrogates for war in the symbolic combat of sports and games. In many ways our adaptations have moved steadily in the direction of peace.

Human females menstruate, which is the same as being in estrus for our primate relatives, but long ago we developed a new use for sexuality: pleasure. There is little pleasure in sexual contact that lasts only a few seconds as it does among most lower primates because one must always be watching out for competing males. We took sex out of public view and made it private. In that way most of the issues of dominance became moot. Other males aren't even around during mating. As for the arousing effect of pheromones, both sexes give them off, and yet we don't claim that women are driven to violence by them. Pheromones give a chemical subtext to sexual attraction, but biologically speaking these chemicals take their place in a complex dance of hormones that has just as much to do with developing healthy organ function as with affecting social behavior. The fact that females want to attract males and vice versa is central to a peaceful society as much as a warring one. We don't equate attraction with fighting.

I could bring up many specifics from animal behavior to support the argument that male dominance is just one factor in how a creature adapts to its environment. It is now known, for instance, that alpha males aren't all that successful. Young males sneak in and breed, too, as they obviously must if the genetic line is to remain strong. I was amused to see how shocked bird-watchers became when it was discovered that the humble English sparrow isn't faithful. Even after pairing off with a single male, female sparrows will invite mating from other males when hubby is away, and hubby is never the wiser. Another sentimental notion has to give way to complex behavior.

Animals cooperate as much, if not more, than they compete. Interdependence is crucial in a balanced ecosystem. Despite the drive to survive, every species has learned how to share territory and food. The lion wants to devour the gazelle, but it can't lie in wait around the watering hole every moment. Lions do better letting the gazelles have a time to drink; otherwise, their prey would all die of thirst. Cuckoos throw out the eggs that belong in another bird's nest to substitute their own, but this behavior is rare. The norm is to respect nesting grounds once they are established. In an extremely intricate way the animal orders have learned that sharing, altruism, and other so-called higher functions have survival benefits. The original Darwinian concept of survival of the fittest ("Nature red in tooth and claw") no longer holds true, if it ever did, as a bald fact. Nature is a dance of adaptations that prove amazingly flexible and ingenious when you really look at them. Evolution is creative. Being ruthless or selfish takes its place alongside countless other behaviors.

If we aren't hard-wired to go to war, why do we choose to? The ethologists can't be entirely wrong. In 1930, near the end of his career, Sigmund Freud published his most pessimistic book, *Civilization and Its Discontents.* It was a time of great social turbulence—Freud would be driven from Vienna by the Nazis in a few years. He had long considered aggression an innate drive. If we were honest with ourselves, he wryly commented, we would admit that nothing could bring more pleasure than to see our enemies hanging from the tallest tree.

But there was an even deeper reason to be pessimistic about the human penchant for violence. In Freud's eyes the mores of society, which are peaceful and cooperative, contradict what our psyche really wants to do, which is to find unlimited outlets for the biological drives of sex and aggression. At the unconscious level, he says, we all act out this contradiction. We are split between what we want to do and what we should do according to a morality that forbids incest, war, sexual promiscuity, and unbridled violence. We try to conform to civilization because it is good for us to live lawfully and at peace with each other, but the primitive drives of the Id (which means "It" in Latin), the part of us that doesn't listen to reason, poses a huge and perhaps insurmountable obstacle to being civilized.

Because he ultimately believed that innate aggression couldn't be overcome, Freud's outlook on the eve of Fascism was especially bleak, yet his brand of determinism holds the same appeal as other deterministic arguments. It carries an air of being objective and scientifically validated. It lets the individual off the hook for having violent behavior because "it" made me do it (think of how automatically we ascribe adolescent behavior to raging hormones). "It" could be genes, the lower brain, Freud's Id, or some other trigger. Determinism is comforting in its simplicity. You can use a slogan like *Men are from Mars, women are from Venus,* and instantly there is a clear-cut explanation for the battle of the sexes.

All deterministic arguments suffer from the same glaring weakness: they don't allow for individuals who break away from the clear prevailing pattern. Without a doubt there are males who aren't aggressive and selfish, and others who understand and empathize with women. There are spiritual people who genuinely transcend violence. Because of that, we are forced to ask, *How did they get that way?* Somehow these people broke through biology, therefore it's not possible to claim that biology determines behavior. Making Leonardo's *Last Supper* a product of biology would sound witless, even though art has primitive roots. It's the same kind of oversimplification to claim that war is attributable to biology. Art and war are complex social creations expressed through individuals, each of whom is a unique blend of biology and many other factors.

Since all cultures produce art, make love, care for their young, worship God, and feel wonder, why should we give dominance to violence just because it is prevalent?

The way of peace doesn't deny biology. It is unarguable that violence is part of our nature. To be honest, you and I have probably been more fascinated by war than we want to admit.

Our brains have absorbed images of piled bodies in Auschwitz and Kurds killed with poison gas in Iraq, children fleeing from napalm in Vietnam and Africans murdered by machetes in Rwanda, an American soldier's corpse being dragged naked and mutilated through the streets of Somalia, and hundreds of other unspeakable outcomes of violence. Those images were metabolized by our cells. Stored as memory, they give us nightmares and stir us to guilt, but they also affect our unconscious mind. But the brain isn't isolated. Every cell is intelligent, and through a constant stream of messenger molecules your heart, liver, and kidneys, not to mention your immune system and endocrine glands, have also absorbed those same horrific images.

It isn't necessary to be on the battle lines to experience the effects of war. Any laboratory experimenter can sit a subject down, expose him to images of war, and detect major changes in every vital sign. You and I have been living in that situation since we were born. When I saw the sickening videos of Daniel Pearl, the *Wall Street Journal* reporter who was kidnapped and ultimately beheaded by jihadists in Pakistan, I felt my heart beat faster with anxiety, and although a rise in blood pressure is normally not something one can subjectively be aware of, I knew that must be happening, too. In many invisible ways my body wasn't at peace anymore. For those moments I was taking on the fearful situation in which this brave captive found himself.

In a more esoteric argument I would suggest that violence pollutes the emotional body, a concept that mainstream medicine wouldn't accept, but it doesn't have to. MRI imaging gives physical evidence that brains exposed to high stress function differently from normal brains—this is true whether the stress is emotional or physical. Brain imaging is just another piece of the puzzle, because evidence had already piled up from studies of hormones that high levels of cortisol and adrenaline (the so-called stress hormones) have a deteriorating effect on the aging process.

In short, the body at peace is not the same as the body at war. When we operate from our war bodies, the world is not the same as when we operate from a body at peace. In the former case we find there is danger and threat everywhere. Stress hormones are catabolic, that is to say, they halt metabolism and break down tissue instead of building it. Bursts of fear, accompanied by a rise in adrenaline, create a steady deteriorating effect. One sees this markedly in the gaunt, gray faces of citizens in any place like Sarajevo where a siege has lasted too long and the body is past its limits of endurance.

The body at war is most damaged whenever three conditions are in force:

The surrounding violence is inescapable.
Bursts of violence come at random.
One has no control over the violence.

It was discovered in the trenches of World War I that combat fatigue isn't a test of character. Every soldier, if exposed long enough to artillery fire and deprived of rest, will become shell-shocked. But in WWI there was always a home front where the shooting stopped. We aren't so fortunate today. Every news story about terrorism reminds us that all three factors exist at home: the threat is inescapable, attacks can come at random, and no individual has control over the outcome. In the film *Fahrenheit 9/11,* the accusation is made that these factors are being manipulated by unscrupulous politicians. The now familiar alert levels from green to yellow, orange, and red are not just alerts; they are a barometer of fear that can be used indiscriminately by the power-hungry.

Since these alert levels get turned into anxiety levels automatically by our bodies, predictably they have lost their effect over time. A kind of civilian battle fatigue has set in, and people who once felt aroused by threat are beginning to find the constancy of threat exhausting. We go through the motions of being on alert while the underlying reality is that alertness is hard to maintain even at minimal levels.

As unwelcome as it would be for the authorities to hear, the body at peace is stronger than the body at war. When you can free yourself of the random, uncontrollable stress that is always present, your body will start to be at peace. Modern medicine has already discovered that love increases the human immune response. An experimenter who showed random subjects a movie of Mother Teresa found that their immune systems responded immediately. The rise of an immunoglobulin called IGA proved that exposure to love actually increased the body's defenses. This happened regardless of whether the subjects approved of Mother Teresa or not. Love, then, has the power to change our bodies as much as violence, but in a positive direction. People who feel loved live longer; have fewer colds, lower blood pressure, and lower cancer rates; and have fewer heart attacks. Widowers who lose a spouse and begin to feel unloved and lonely suffer higher rates of all these afflictions, as well as a shorter life span. You cannot use stress, in the form of constant reminders about terror, to create peace in the body. The mechanisms simply aren't there.

PUTTING THE BODY AT PEACE

Don't dwell on stressful events.

Avoid becoming addicted to bad news.

Put fear in perspective.

Realize that positive outcomes are possible.

Discuss how you feel with others; work together to change the
stress.

Be in control where you can. Don't let chaos dominate.

Stay centered, and whenever you are thrown off center, take
time to return there.

Find an outlet for your anger and anxiety.

These are common-sense suggestions, but I wonder how many
people use them. For every lunch meeting where two friends fret
over living in a time of war and terror, there should be one where
they speculate about the best way to find peace. In a time of crisis,
putting your body at peace can seem like a full-time job. A friend
of mine spoke to me about it. "I was sleeping late when 9/11
occurred. I woke up that day to phone messages that sounded
hysterical, and when I turned on the television, I got pulled into
the scenes of chaos and destruction. Yet somehow I felt immune.
After twenty years of meditating, I could empathize with the hor-
rible feelings that people were having, but I was proud that I
could stand apart to send healing light and energy to them rather
than crying with them.

"Gradually this state changed. I became a cable news junkie.
I exposed myself to every detail of the war in Afghanistan. I followed the plight of the victims' families after 9/11 and listened to
every word of the tapes from the jet that was downed over Penn-
sylvania, as well as phone messages left by people in the twin towers who knew they were going to die.

"I craved this information. I wanted to be plugged in. But
then things began to happen that I didn't want. I started to buy into
the negative feelings, obsessing about revenge fantasies against
those terrorist bastards. The idea of going to war got me pumped.

"Did all those years of meditation count for nothing? No,
but like anyone else I have to fight the darkness. Once I noticed

what was happening, I pulled out. I'm not a war junkie anymore, and it's amazing to see people running around who are. They look unreal to me. I guess my only advantage over most people is that I know that I can't let darkness win, and my spiritual vision tells me that it won't."

Spiritual life is all about finding a center and holding on to it. Negativity can feel like your center. If you grimly hold on to a belief that this is war and our evil enemies must be exterminated, that core of determination is real psychologically, but it isn't your core.

You must confront the fact that not just your body, but the body politic is affected by violence. When you find yourself fixated on war and violence you are empathically drawing in what others feel. This osmosis isn't unhealthy per se. Collective consciousness is part of you. But it isn't your real self, and if you mistake what others feel for what you feel, you are putting your body at war for a bad reason; because everyone else is doing it.

My friend who got sucked into war hysteria reversed the process: he realized that there was no value in keeping up with daily negative developments. He went back to asking himself how he really wanted to feel. Whatever others might experience, he personally experienced war as a stress, a negative condition that nobody was forcing him into. So he stopped participating in the war mentality.

To say all this isn't the same as going through it. You have to put your own body at peace, and then, in the absence of turmoil, you can find out what you want to hold on to. Spirituality without a core of peace is very limited.

Recently I met a man who had remarkable gifts of healing. He didn't have to touch people afflicted with illness. If he simply pointed his finger they would often begin to tremble, see a rush of inner light, and lose the strength to stand up. Those are known to be classic symptoms of faith healing. This man seemed to be able to make illness go away, however one explains it. But when it came to war he told me stoutly that he supported preemptive strikes against terrorist countries and firmly believed that Iraq had weapons of mass destruction, which they cannily hid in advance of the war. "I'm voting for Bush because he's the most likely one to keep us safe," he said, echoing the words of political ads more than the thoughts of a person who has confronted his own darkness.

Enough people already side with killing the enemy. Belligerence and fear don't need your help, in case you thought we were in imminent danger of an outbreak of peace. Even if nuclear weapons have to be forced out of North Korea or Iran down the line, the body at peace is still worth having. It can serve as the vehicle for bringing the world back to sanity. The bedrock argument here is that the body at peace is normal, whereas the body at war is not.

OUR BEST HOPE

WHAT DO YOU do in a hopeless situation? How can hope
come to your aid once again? The way of peace has to
answer these questions. Hope is emotionally necessary in a crisis.
It's one of the chief ways our minds protect us. Yet hope has a
hard time being felt when every disaster is instantly communicated
around the world. And hope is rarely pure. It is always mixed
in the tangled hierarchy with other emotions, including those
opposed to hope, such as despair, fear, anger, and vengeance.

Because of this tangle, hope has often been a cloak for violence. How many times have we heard politicians, on the eve of
war, seize the microphone to express how fervently they hope for
peace? One must pay lip service to hope even when an enemy is
being driven into hopelessness and crushed without mercy.

We have lost touch with the reality of hope, which is a powerful force when it has a spiritual source but a deception when it
doesn't. To show what I mean, let me relate a story of medical
hope. I met a cancer patient recently who felt himself to be in
good health until he found it hard one day to come up with the

right words when he wanted to say something. His speech became slurred enough for others to notice, and then one day he stumbled against a wall, unable to keep his balance while walking across the room. He was rushed to the hospital, an MRI was taken, and a few hours later he learned that he was suffering from a massive brain tumor.

The surgeons went in, but when they saw the malignancy, they closed up his skull without removing the tumor. The man had a glial blastoma, the fastest growing and most deadly form of brain cancer. His tumor had already spread beyond the original mass, infiltrating more than one region of the brain.

"When I got the news, everyone was in tears, and I could feel panic in the room," he recounts. "For some reason I wasn't panicked. I asked my family for only one thing, that they believe I wouldn't leave them. Shakily they agreed to this and left. I lay in the hospital bed alone, and my mind was very quiet. The only thought I had was *How am I going to get out of this one?*".

"At that moment I noticed a brightness out of the corner of my eye. It was coming from the far corner of the room, and as I watched it became brighter and brighter. I saw the form of a woman surrounded by faces. I seemed to know who these faces were, and they seemed to know me, but I couldn't put names to them. The woman told me that I would be all right. After she said this the light began to fade and was gone.

"For the first time in several nights I was able to sleep, and when I woke up I felt stronger. The morning nurse came in and I told her I had seen an apparition. She said, 'I'm just here to take your pulse,' so it occurred to me that I might want to keep this experience to myself. I decided to send my MRI to every cancer center I could find, but they all refused to treat me. Most said that my best course was to go home, buy some diapers, and wait for the end.

"Finally I got a specialist on brain and spinal tumors to agree to see me. Even he made me wait two weeks, no doubt expecting that I wouldn't live to make the appointment. But when we met he put me on a new chemotherapy that might cause my blastoma to stop growing and at best remain the size it already was. Nothing was promised, but inside I felt I didn't need promises.

"I went on a month's course of pills that cost twenty-five thousand dollars. For some reason I had few or no side effects. When they took the next MRI, my tumor had vanished. Everyone was shocked and amazed. Other patients with my condition had died despite the new drug; fewer than one in seventeen thousand survives six months. I'm happy to report that I am four months beyond that six months, and although still being treated, I feel more hopeful than ever."

When hope serves as a means to reach deeper into yourself than anyone could predict, or than anyone believes possible, it is a spiritual force. This story has certain hallmarks of similar cases of remarkable recoveries:

The person is without fear.

There is belief in an extraordinary outcome.

The search for a cure doesn't depend on outside opinions.

Often there is an unshakable certainty that a cure will be found.

These same qualities apply to any situation that is considered hopeless by the majority of observers. To rekindle hope, one must find a path to the extraordinary. This requires a shift in oneself, for we have all become used to a much weaker kind of hope. Consider these two sentences:

My husband beat me again last night, but I hope he won't do it anymore.

My mother was an alcoholic, and I remember hoping desperately that she would stop.

What reactions come to mind as you read these words? I

imagine that most people would immediately react with sadness and sympathy, but others especially if they have been in similar predicaments would feel a surge of anger. One might also have negative judgments about passivity and co-dependence. Simply to hope that an alcoholic will get better, we now know, is a way of enabling the addiction, just as hoping that an abuser will stop hurting you is the same as making yourself a victim.

Fifty years ago the best-trained therapists didn't tell families of alcoholics to quit enabling them, and women who suffered from domestic violence were told to stay in the marriage for the sake of the children. Today therapists say almost the opposite, even though it has taken a long time for the police to do anything about a man who beats his wife except to look the other way.

Violence especially needs to be treated with hope because at bottom a violent person is hopeless. One reads of the "black widows" in Chechnya and other Muslim women around the world who are willing to become suicide bombers. How should we feel about these women? The way we view them says a lot about our own awareness. The most common view is to deplore them as the worst of terrorists; they are irrational fanatics sold out to a religion that promises paradise as a reward for martyrdom. The next most common reaction is to see them as bizarrely misdirected in their faith. This view comes from those who still maintain that Islam is a peaceful religion that condemns suicide and makes it a sin to kill innocent people. On the battlefront I'm sure these women are objects of intense fear. To a young American soldier the sight of veiled women in black, each looking almost identical to the next, carries the potential that all of them could be suicide bombers. That is why some innocent Iraqi women have been shot as they drove into American checkpoints past the posted stop signs. The excuse that they couldn't read the signs, or that the verbal commands to halt were in garbled Arabic, is too weak. Better to shoot them than to take a chance that they are among the irrational fanatics.

The least common view is that these women have lost all hope. As with gang violence in the ghetto, the hopeless among us belong to a subculture, and the behavior of that subculture has a life on its own. One of the most violent gang leaders in Los Angeles was infamous for amputating the limbs of rival gang members while they were being held down on the ground. Eventually "Monstah," as he was known, was captured by the police and sent to maximum-security prison for life. He turned out to be an intelligent person from a less-than-impoverished background. But his father had deserted the family before he was born, and life in South Central L.A. taught young Kody Scott—his real name—that he could only survive by becoming the most brutal male in a subculture where drugs, police harassment, and the law of the jungle were daily norms.

For Monstah, violence became a way to assert power and gain status. It worked for a few years as he rose to "ghetto superstardom," and then reached a predictable end. He was a sociopath, given to not the slightest hint of remorse for his murders. But what allowed a sociopath to become a model of status, power, and respect among his peers? The answer is the unquestionable hopelessness that was a given in that environment. In many parts of the world hopelessness is a daily fact. Palestine, the Sudan, Colombia (a country that continues to have the highest murder rate in the world despite massive infusions of American money and military assistance), and Rwanda come to mind immediately.

Just as the tangled hierarchy has made ordinary Americans fashion a normal life around the ghastly weapons we developed and the horrific possibility that they might be used against us, ordinary people in these places must fashion normal lives around hopelessness. That's how hope gets turned on its head. It can shield a problem and make it worse. No doubt one of the most difficult emotions to face is hopelessness, and yet you have to face it if you want to understand hope itself. Consider these two sentences:

My whole family was killed in Bosnia, but I hope the fighting will end.

My father is teaching me to make bombs, but I hope I never have to blow myself up.

These statements sound painfully futile. They aren't extreme or imaginary, however. Someone trapped by violence is thinking them right now. In the late 1980s Europe and the United States stood by and allowed tens of thousands of Bosnians to be raped and killed, hoping that diplomacy and international pressure would end the Serbs' policy of ethnic cleansing. Isn't that a misuse of hope?

The trick here is not to despair, and yet since we despair so quickly in our current condition, avoiding despair can only happen by going deeper into the spiritual value of hope. The Sufi mystic and teacher Meher Baba once remarked, "The only prerequisite for enlightenment is complete disillusion." Illusion keeps us in the grip of denial. It coaxes us to rely on our false friends instead of our true ones. If you can see with open eyes when hope is a false friend, you are moving ahead spiritually, because spirit doesn't need hope once it can have reality instead.

HOPE IS A FALSE FRIEND

When it is a mask for denial.

When it is the same as apathy.

When it papers over conflicts.

When it coerces people to suffer in silence.

When it enables victimhood.

When it prevents realization.

All these conditions tend to hang together, and yet they are often too subtle for most people to notice. I have a friend who grew up in a prosperous family. As a child he was sensitive and mature beyond his years. His mother likes to say that at six he was like a small adult. He excelled in school, eventually graduating from an Ivy League college and moving on to a successful career. He had learned quickly as a child that something wasn't quite right at home, and the problem centered around his father.

"I went to sleep at night hearing him mumble as he passed out, and I woke up many mornings hearing him unscrew the top of a vodka bottle. I didn't take these to be normal. I knew something was warped about his outbursts of anger and the distance that couldn't be bridged between my father and everyone else. But it was only when I turned ten that my mother confessed to me that we had a little family secret: Daddy drank too much.

"From that moment on a curtain fell over my heart. I formed an abiding hatred for my father and intense sympathy for my mother. She wasn't strong, but she had the qualities of loving patience and quiet acceptance. Because this was her way of dealing with the problem I followed her lead, or tried to. I couldn't find any real reason to love my father, yet I learned to be good.

"And goodness paid off. I grew up and got out of the house. I succeeded. I began eventually to build a family of my own. One small thing I was most proud of, though. I could keep alcohol around the house and not abuse it. You would never know that I came from the background of an alcoholic."

My friend followed the lead of his mother's hope, a woman who had no other tools at her disposal. But in fact hope was a false friend, a realization that only hit home years later.

"I had gone one day to have a tooth extracted. I was thirty-two at the time. I wasn't feeling particularly nervous. There was no pain, and the dead tooth had to come out. But as the dentist and his assistant leaned over me, their heads almost touching as they filled my field of vision, they morphed into the faces of my father and mother.

"Suddenly I knew that I had been the victim of a collusion. My bad father and my good mother had joined forces without me ever suspecting. At that instant I was hit by an unthinkable thought: these two people stole my childhood. They could have tried harder to nurture me, they could have tried harder to know me. But they didn't. They chose to steal from me instead. It was all I could do to keep my grief from overflowing right there in the dentist's chair, so strongly did I see the truth of these facts. It was a truth I couldn't change, but far worse for me, it was a truth nobody else in my family—the very people who say they loved me the most—would ever, ever admit."

In this story I see the courage of someone who could face up to false hope and then emerge with real hope, the kind founded on self-knowledge. The moment of realization was painful but decisive in its ability to liberate him.

The best hope in any situation follows certain principles.

THE BEST HOPE

Unmasks denial.
Inspires an end to apathy.
Faces up to conflict.
Brings an end to silent suffering.
Changes the situation of victims.
Brings about realization.

The way of peace includes all these things, and if anyone wants to bring hope to a place like Iraq or Sudan or Colombia, following these principles will work.

Unmasking denial

Denial is the general belief that things will improve if one does nothing. It is not a simple mechanism, however. Are we in denial to believe that Palestinians and Israelis can live together, or is that the best hope and worthy of being pursued? Are we in denial that the Middle East can be freed of fanatic religionists who control the dialogue in every country, or is that a vision of the future we must keep alive? There is no fixed answer anyone can seize on as the truth. But if we strip away denial, hope has a chance.

It's denial to say that your side of a dispute is always right and the other side always wrong.

It's denial to pretend that you are fearless.

It's denial to claim that you are willing to pay any price in blood to get what you want.

It's denial to act as if the other side doesn't exist and has no right to speak.

It's denial to say that you have nothing in common with your enemy.

War persists because nations hide behind these denials. Giving in to common humanity is considered too difficult. One nation would have to say to another, I am as afraid as you are. I know we fight because we want the same thing, but neither of us is going to get it. We have to feel for each other and see if our differences can be settled. Diplomats might want to say such things, but they know it would be career suicide if they did. Denial keeps going because it masquerades as strength. A truism in therapy is that what you don't acknowledge can't be understood, and what you don't understand can't be healed. When a country postures as being tough and strong, admitting no weakness, giving no quarter, the short-term result may be a boost in confidence, but the long-term result is more violence. As I write,

President Putin is demanding a sweeping increase in power in the ongoing crisis with Chechnya. He has suppressed the free press, reined in opposing opinions at the state-run television, arrested foes of his economic reforms, and promises to crush any rebellious action against Moscow as terrorism or some other crime. This is an extreme example of how denial leads to desperate measures, for the argument that violence must be met every step of the way with more violence has proved disastrous throughout history. The one thing Putin refuses to admit—that the enemy has legitimate complaints—is the one thing that must emerge from the cloak of denial if the cycle of violence has a prayer of ending.

What you resist persists; what you feel, you can heal.

Inspiring an end to apathy

Apathy has been seen as a moral failing or a refusal to do your duty. Apathetic voter turnout, for example, is blamed for the excessive power of splinter groups like the fundamentalist Christian right at its worst. Most often, however, apathy is a symptom of being overwhelmed. If you place a white rat on a plate that emits an electrical charge, administering a mild shock every few minutes, the animal at first will react sharply. It will jump at the shock and frantically try to get away. But if you keep applying the shocks, its efforts to escape will grow weak and erratic. Eventually you can administer all the shocks you want, at any volume of pain. The rat will lie still and not move at all.

The shock of modern violence has created the same effect in us. Vietnam was famously the first televised war. With images of death and havoc staring us in the face, no one could *not* react. But the images never stopped, and intermittently they were too terrible to take in (such as the heartrending photo of a naked

Vietnamese girl running down the road screaming from a na-palm attack). One of the tenets that underlies Eastern thought is that each person has an emotional body, and like our physical bodies, this one can be scarred. Scars in the physical body prevent the growth of new tissue; they have stopped short of true healing, which lets in new life and new growth.

These repeated images of horror have badly scarred our emotional bodies, and like the rats on the electrical plate, we no longer react, no matter how strong the next charge may be. The rest of the psyche organizes around the scarred tissue, just as skin keeps growing around a battle scar. When pictures of torture emerged from the Abu Ghraib prison in Iraq, I was startled by the absence of deep emotional reaction. People acted shocked, taken aback, dismayed, disbelieving, outraged, and appalled. But this discomfort didn't translate into the abiding shame and pain that followed the photos of the German concentration camps after they were liberated in 1945. Not that the two are equal as crimes, but in both cases a moral person would feel the same deep grief for betrayed humanity.

It is part of the way of peace to be freshly hurt each time humanity is betrayed. Apathy, in the form of emotional numbness, must be healed in order for this to happen. Just as with victims of extreme domestic abuse, an emotional body that has been scarred through war can persist in a state of hopelessness. You and I were not present during the slaughter in Cambodia or Rwanda, but our emotional bodies give those events a presence inside ourselves. *"If you do it to the least, you do it to me"* is the guiding principle here. Hope enters as a healing tool to say that humanity can be betrayed but never forgotten. Hope is the hand that reaches out to say, *I feel who you are and what is happening to you.*

Facing up to conflict

Many spiritual people believe that conflict is always to be shunned. They disapprove of it morally; in their minds every conflict is a form of violence. Yet inner conflict is present in everyone. We are driven by contradictory feelings and ideas. At times the contradictions are painful. You want to see yourself as a good person, yet you have impulses that no good person (as you define it) should ever have. You want to see your country as a good country, but it has impulses no good country should ever have. There is very little difference between those two states.

Most violence in this world isn't committed by bad people. It is committed by people who are expressing what's inside themselves, and if what is inside is rage and fear, the very effort to keep these feelings down will eventually be the cause of their eruption. I've said that all wars are eruptions from the unconscious. The conflict that gets all the headlines is international war, but the inner war inside each individual is actually more important. It is the seed from which all other conflicts grow.

Of course, our leaders refuse to admit any of this. Politicians are under immense pressure to appear to be what they are not—certain, stable, and decisive at every moment. In other words, unconflicted. This form of public deception is unhealthy for everyone. The common excuse for the politician's facade of unwavering strength is that the public demands strong leaders. No less a personage than former president Bill Clinton paid an enormous price in humiliation and shame as a result of not admitting that he had weaknesses. In his autobiography he details the sexual misadventures that hounded his career from the outset, born of impulses he could not control. But impulses are only uncontrollable when one ignores them until it is too late and they begin to erupt on their own.

When he went into therapy to examine why he had publicly destroyed his good reputation, Clinton discovered the concept of "splitting." This term describes a tactic of the psyche: when we have desires that are so bad or shameful that our official self totally rejects them, they get split off into a region that has no contact with the rest of the personality. Many kinds of extreme behavior fit into this category. Murderous rage, of the kind that propels serial killers, or psychopathic sexual violence, such as crops up in serial rapists, is split off so completely that the person appears, if anything, milder and nicer than average.

Once split off, these energies of the psyche don't lie dormant. They are part of ourselves, therefore they can think, feel, and talk to us. Like neglected children, they want attention, and the more we ignore them, the louder their demands become. In Clinton's case, the acting out became increasingly tawdry, finally creeping into the Oval Office, the very place where the official self was supposed to be at its best. The split energies knew that. They knew that a president is supposed to be strong, disciplined, a model of self-control. What better way, then, to show that another part of the psyche was wild, self-indulgent, and out of control?

Nobody is immune from splitting, although it may be extremely well masked. You don't have to be a Jekyll and Hyde, the classic parable of splitting. I was fascinated to read how the noted Swiss psychotherapist Alice Miller realized the power of her own inner conflict. She was an apparently healthy person, psychologically speaking, having trained as a therapist and undergone two courses of complete psychoanalysis. This certainly meant that she had examined and cleared away all the tangled underbrush of her unconscious mind. Then she happened to enroll in art classes where the teacher encouraged the students to bring forth, without censorship, any images that wanted to emerge. They were to paint as freely as possible, not judging against any image for being too strange, scary, or inappropriate. To her astonishment, Miller found that the images pouring from her brush were very violent. They showed fanged figures trapped behind bars. On their faces were expressions of torment. As these disturbing images came to light, fully equivalent to those that might be painted in a mental asylum, Miller began to flash back to childhood scenes that supposedly had been worked though in her years of therapy. They were in fact far from that. They were still full of psychic charges, replete with anger and hurt. The fanged prisoners in her pictures were herself.

If this is true of someone with so much insight and intelligence, I don't think any of us can leap to the conclusion that we are completely nonviolent inside. We may not act out our violence, having turned it into acceptable behavior or made it entirely absent from our daily lives. But the fact that the world displays so much violence means that our own hidden conflict has found a way to picture itself outwardly.

The way of peace brings us to inner truth by one road or another. Alice Miller was brought there by seeing undeniable evidence of her inner demons. You and I may find our truths differently, through depression, sadness, outbursts of anger, a nagging conscience, or sheer courage. There is hope that any conflict can end once you reach its source. Conflict is the inevitable result of separation. It isn't your fault or your shame. Conflict even has a necessary place in the journey of the soul. It serves as the meeting point between two choices, and as long as we are on the path, choice is a constant. There isn't a single choice you can make once and for all. The journey is too dynamic for that, and the deepest drives return time and again at different stages of life. Hope tells us that every conflict is serving spirit,

even in those dark days when we are tempted to believe that con‐
flict is only here to defeat us.

Bringing an end to silent suffering

The moral view of violence, labeling it as bad and wrong, has
done little to end it. The alternative view is to release our judg‐
ments and see violence for what it is: a form of suffering. This is
a difficult shift for many people. Not only are they in the habit of
making knee-jerk judgments, but violent people cause harm, and
therefore their suffering seems to deserve less sympathy. *You hurt
me, so why should I have compassion for you? It should be the other way around.*
Does it take a saint to make the shift from moral outrage to com‐
passion?

I think of the Bishop of Digne in Victor Hugo's *Les Misérables*
who gives shelter and food to the starving, hounded convict Jean
Valjean. In return for this kindness Valjean steals the bishop's
silver. When he is caught by the police and returned to face the
victim of his crime, Valjean is certain he will be returned to the
prison that had stripped him of all hope and faith. Instead the
bishop seconds his alibi that the pair of precious silver candle‐
sticks found by the police was a gift. Then he utters the decisive
lines in the novel: "You belong no longer to evil, but to good. It
is your soul that I am buying from you. I withdraw it from dark
thoughts, and from the spirit of perdition. I give it to God!"

What makes this scene so moving is that it pertains not just to a
desperate criminal but to everyone's soul journey. Turning points
arrive when we can make a choice not to suffer in silence. We then
strike a soul bargain that is fearful but necessary. The bargain is
that redemption is possible through love. The absence of love is
absolutely the problem, and love is absolutely the solution. We
don't have to couch this truth in religious terms. We do not have to

reach into another realm to locate the redeeming power of love that is available to us here and now.

The problem is that love comes through a fallible human being. Figures of unblemished kindness like the fictional Bishop of Digne are inspiring, but it's not enough merely to mechanically imitate them. (Kindness carried out as a ritual, a habit, or a duty has its place. I would rather see every beggar on the street get a handout than to see them be met with scorn and contempt.) But decisive kindness, the one act that saves a soul the way Jean Valjean is saved, isn't the rule. The rule is constant work on the spiritual path to clear away the obstacles that prevent love from coming through us. The work is much more like working on clogged plumbing than it is like imitating a saint.

Hope is the emotion that sustains this dogged work even when results seem to be slow or impossible. Can I love the terrorist who harms my country? Can I love the criminal who wants to harm me? At the level of the soul I already do, and the spiritual path is a means to arrive at that level. Because the soul doesn't live in a place, the metaphor of journeying isn't really accurate. What's accurate is the process of change. No one is required to leap into sudden compassion for terrorists, or even to announce publicly that our enemies deserve love. But in our souls each of us harbors the knowledge that only love is going to bring violence to an end. No matter how you and I live our outward lives, our spiritual lives must remain devoted to that vision.

Changing the situation of victims

One situation that needs constant address, day after day, is that of the victim. Buried in the back of my mind is a sentence I read over thirty years ago, which said that anger is the result of the conviction of injustice. Very philosophical wording for a simple notion: When we feel that life is unfair to us, we respond with anger. Victims come in various shades of anger. Some are in a state of loud-voiced righteous outrage. Others are worn out, exhausted by a smoldering anger that will never be answered and old wrongs that will never be righted. In between these poles of outrage and exhaustion normal life goes on. But normal life is also rife with victimization. People walk around every day harboring a set of beliefs that keep them stuck in their status as victims:

THE VICTIM'S BELIEF SYSTEM

What you have to face before you can recover

I'm completely innocent, I don't deserve this.
There was nothing I could do about it.
Someone else is to blame.
People are just cruel sometimes.
Life is unfair.
I want to get back in control, but it's hard.
I have to be on guard all the time now.
It could happen again, but I won't let it.
There's almost nothing I can do about this fear.

The recovery movement is now mature enough as a social force that this list of beliefs won't come as any surprise. However, we have become too accustomed to seeing victims through their own eyes. They believe these tenets with all their heart, and that makes it harder to see past the trauma. For many victims their traumas give them purpose. In a strange way being wounded becomes their life, as a disease can become the whole life of a chronic invalid. We know it's not healthy for an invalid to turn into his disease; it's equally unhealthy for a victim to turn into his trauma.

Yet it happens, often without warning. The noted psychiatrist Irvin Yalom writes of an older, well-to-do woman whose life had no apparent disturbance. She was happy and healthy until the night she went out to a restaurant with her husband. In the parking lot a random mugger grabbed her purse and ran off. He was never caught; the purse was never recovered. This isn't an uncommon occurrence in any large city, yet the consequences for this woman were remarkable.

She couldn't forget the incident. Instead of growing fainter with time, it became magnified. She began to feel deeply violated, and over the next few months, some part of herself was stolen: her sense of being invulnerable. Unknown to herself, this was a key part of her makeup psychologically, as it is for all of us. More than one spiritual master has said that we must live every day as if death is stalking us constantly, for in fact that is true. But our psyches are organized around the very opposite idea, that we will never be hurt, grow sick, and die.

Beneath the surface we all know these truths to be self-evident. Even so, we don't accept them. Growing sick and dying is always happening to somebody else. The spiritual masters who want us to be aware of mortality aren't sadists. They just believe that if we turn our backs on the truth, it will never be able to liberate us. That is why going through the trauma is finally the only solution to victimhood. The simplest definition of a victim is this: someone who can't stop being hurt.

Which is exactly how this woman began to relate. Intensely depressed, she became frightened of everything. The slightest threat, or even suggestion of a threat, sent her into a paroxysm of terror. In effect she became her own terrorist, for it's the hallmark of terrorism to make everyday life appear fatally dangerous. In her words, she had lost the sense of being special, which to her meant being safe and protected from the harms that come to other, less special people.

The answer for her was long-term therapy, but I've brought in her story because it illustrates the insidious nature of the victim's belief system. There is no doubt that the facts seem to support all the beliefs I've listed. If someone randomly commits violence against you, the facts seem to scream that life is unfair, you are innocent, random human cruelty took away your sense of self-control.

But despite all that, what's really happening is that you have shifted into relating to the world through a trauma. It isn't the trauma itself that caused this shift. There had to be readiness inside. In truth life is neither fair nor unfair. The world is a reflection of who we are inside.

I came face to face with this recently in an encounter that left me filled with an eerie kind of wonder. At a social event in a distant city I was introduced to a married couple in their eighties. They were originally Czech, and we hit it off when I expressed my admiration for Vaclav Havel, the former president of Czechoslovakia (now the Czech Republic), who is a remarkable spiritual figure.

The old couple smiled and nodded their heads, and watching their faces I realized that there was something different about them. They radiated a calm light that seemed both peaceful and full of joy. It came time for me to leave, and in the car afterward my host said, "I'm glad you liked them so much. They met in Auschwitz, you know."

I was stunned. Seeing the look on my face, my host told me their story. They were both Jewish and had been rounded up with other Czech Jews around 1943. The man was a baker by profession, then only in his early twenties, but the Nazis needed bakers, and he was allowed to live. Months passed, and he would never have survived except that the work of mass killing couldn't be finished before the advancing Allies arrived. The woman survived mostly because she was such a late arrival that she had not been fully processed, and being young and healthy she was also exploited as a worker.

I couldn't match these horrific facts with the two people I had just met. They didn't wear their history out in the open; indeed, they never referred to it. I longed to ask them if their experience in the camps had led to their current state of peace, by an act of alchemy that the psyche is certainly capable of when it confronts the deepest horror. Or had they been this way before? Or did it take years of conscious forgetting to work through their trauma?

I will never know, yet I do know one thing: if you can stop relating to the world through your trauma, there is hope that you can begin to relate through your soul. Here is how the process needs to go.

Victims hang on to their status because they feel innocent. The husband who suddenly announces that he wants a divorce and has found a new woman to love, the mugger who pulls a gun or knife on a dark street as you step out of your car, the highway accident that kills a member of your family: none of these events has a justified cause. They become imprinted in the mind as a wound. This wound is the problem. It always hurts. It always takes time to recover from. It always results in tears and anxiety that one felt immune to beforehand.

Yet in some ways a psychic wound is very different from a physical one. If you are not vigilant, it turns into part of your identity, and then the danger of relating to the world through this wound becomes sharper. Victims can't find enough strength to keep their identities from shifting. As with the woman whose purse was snatched, it's as if an invading virus has entered the system and can't be stopped. It corrupts the everyday sense of being happy, special, and protected.

This is all to say that the specific idea *I am innocent* is a blind, a mask. Yes, you are innocent. The attack against your sense of self has no justification. But only a stronger sense of self is going to rescue you. Your mind will never resolve why you, of all people, got hurt. Its struggles are futile from the outset. I've met people who spend years in an attempt to figure out whether their misfortunes are due to bad karma. This becomes the magical word for a twisted logic that says "I didn't think I deserved to be hurt, but if you look at a deeper, more mystical layer, I did."

This isn't really an answer. First of all, it doesn't heal the wound. Secondly, it exists as a mental construct and does little to salve the emotions, which are the chief fuel for ongoing victimization. You *feel* victimized, regardless of what your mind says. So even if you wholeheartedly believe that there is a deeper level of guilt that cancels out your innocence, what have you understood? That every action is both guilty and innocent? Such doublethink strikes me as the essence of confusion and futility.

The whole package—the event itself, the wound, the feelings that erupt, and the mind's scramble to find an explanation—is so interwoven that it cannot be untangled. If you can face this fact, you have come a long way to understanding how life works. This doesn't mean you can't heal the wound. In fact, realizing that reality is tangled serves you in your healing, because you can stop yourself from pursuing the false hope that everything will one day be revealed and straightened out.

True hope offers something different. You can recover. Obsessing over guilt and innocence is perhaps inescapable; we all do it a great deal of the time after bad things happen to us. But there is a deeper truth, which is that the soul has a clear vision of the way out. You have to know this in advance to take advantage of it. Yes, the world is a tangled hierarchy, but the very phrase implies that there is something at the top of the hierarchy. That something is absolute consciousness, the pure state of being. Its essence is your essence. Its intelligence is your intelligence. Its clarity and ability to organize life are yours, also. The victim has lost touch with these truths. Victimhood will end immediately once they come back into awareness. The path of healing brings them back, step by step. With that in mind, hope is the assurance that your connection to pure Being can never be lost; the worst trauma in the world can't harm Being by a single scratch.

Bringing about realization

As best I can, I am trying to link the crucial things that hope can do. Emotions can be healed, gradually, so that they no longer feel numbed by past traumas. Your beliefs can be changed by seriously examining what they have to say. Yet eventually there has to be a step that makes your new reality hang together as solidly as your old reality.

That step is realization.

Realization carries a magical power, akin to insight but much deeper. You suddenly *know* that you are the author of your own life. You can gather the power of change around you. Realization, or its absence, affects everyone's life. Every doctor is struck by how peculiarly people react to their diagnoses. The same symptoms can lead to astonishingly varied results. This is particularly mysterious in the case of cancer. Some of the most virulent malignancies, such as melanoma, the most deadly of skin cancers, also have the highest rates of spontaneous remission.

I've witnessed that, and also its opposite. I had a patient years ago, a young woman with a suspicious shadow on her lung

X-ray. The shadow was consistent with lung cancer, but by no means was it definitive. The young woman was devastated by the news, however. She went into a rapid decline and within months died from lung cancer. Yet a retrospective examination of her earlier X-rays, going back more than five years, disclosed that the same shadow had been present then and showed little signs of growth. Her previous physician had either not told her of the shadow or had minimized its significance.

The inescapable conclusion is that the cancer spread rapidly only after the patient became aware of its danger. In short, she died of her diagnosis. In medicine this would be considered an extreme form of a well-known phenomenon called control by the host. Each of us is exposed to countless disease organisms every day, some of which are defeated by the immune system, some get past our defenses and make us sick, and some simply live inside us as unnoticed guests. Given this fact, how do germs sort out which ones are going to cause problems and which aren't? Apparently the decision is made by the body itself. The host somehow controls which disease is going to flourish and which isn't.

Until we know how control by the host works (and science is far from that point) it can only be said that the whole patient is involved. People die all the time because they want to; they survive all the time because they don't want to die. I remember as a young resident one devoted couple that was admitted into the hospital with cancer. The husband's condition was much worse than the wife's, but he hung on week after week. Despite the relative difference in her disease, the wife died first. Within twenty-four hours so did the husband. I know that he consciously waited for her, because he actually told me indirectly when he said, one day on my rounds, that a gentleman always holds the door for a lady. And so he did.

Spiritual realization is very much like control by the host. At some level we all know everything, because we are nothing except pure consciousness. We know who loves us and who doesn't. We know that there is equality among human beings, that there is a reality beyond the physical, that nothing happens by chance. Those shining moments that get labeled as epiphanies happen when we permit ourselves to know what we already know.

In the blazing Aha! of realization life becomes more real, not so much because it changed but because we decided to relate to it differently. Fortunately, this isn't just a mood swing. In the tangled hierarchy, certain powers are only unveiled when you give yourself permission to tap into them.

If hope is your guiding beacon, you must be willing to view it metaphysically. Rumi, the most assured of metaphysical poets, says, "There is a field beyond right and wrong. Come, and I will meet you there." In India this is called Vedanta. Veda is the truth, the good life as handed down from God, but all the good in the world can't make it a peaceful place. We have had goodness for a long time, and yet the world is a sinkhole of violence, intolerance, famine, war, and greed. Vedanta means the end of the Veda, in other words, looking beyond goodness. You may call this a form of radical hope, and I would agree, but what will make it a reality?

Realizing that only spiritual solutions will work.

These solutions only come about with a change in consciousness.

A change in consciousness happens one person at a time.

There is a spiritual law which states that we must celebrate our losses, for only the unreal can be lost, and once it is gone, the real remains. Hence Meher Baba's apparently cynical (but in fact very wise) advice that the way to enlightenment is through total disillusion. The key word is *total*. If you intend to change your consciousness so completely that violence is extinguished, you will no longer be an ego-driven personality. You will have no stake in politics or psychology or money or the future. Your only stake will be in the timeless region where consciousness is born. Find that seed ground, and every day that you touch it, even lightly, you will add to the peace of the world in a way that no other action can hope to do. At one level you will remain the concerned citizen, the doer of good, the person full of hope. But at a deeper level you will keep your eyes on the absolute as the only begetter of transformation here on earth.

Epilogue

HAVE YOU HEARD the Buddhist fable of Sticky Hair and Prince Five Weapons?

Sticky Hair was a monster, a giant ogre who lived deep in the woods in India. He fed off the villagers beyond the woods and kept them in a state of constant terror. One day a hero appeared on the scene to rescue them. He went by the curious name of Prince Five Weapons. When he was born the court astrologers gathered around his cradle. They predicted that the baby would grow up to become a mighty warrior, the master of not one weapon but five. Armed with his five weapons the prince set out to defeat the monster.

When the two of them met in the woods, the prince took out his bow and arrow and fired a volley into the ogre's side, but Sticky Hair's thick mat of fur was impenetrable, and every arrow uselessly stuck to him. The prince pulled out his sword and hacked at the ogre, but his sword too got stuck in the sticky fur, along with the prince's knife, club, and pike.

With his five weapons gone, the prince leapt onto the beast with his fists, but in a flash his hands and feet were also caught in

Sticky Hair's fur. The monster would have eaten him immediately, but Prince Five Weapons' courage gave him pause. "If this hero can fight so bravely against me, maybe I'd better think this thing over," Sticky Hair mused.

The prince was doomed, then suddenly he had a flash. "You don't dare eat me," he shouted defiantly. "All my weapons may be stuck to you, but I have a secret inside me. As soon as you swallow me up it will explode, and then you will die."

Sticky Hair was impressed, and not wanting to die, he let Prince Five Weapons go. But before he left, the monster wanted to know what the hidden secret was. "Is it a sixth weapon I've never seen?"

"It is no weapon at all, but compassion," said the prince, who was well versed in the wisdom of the Buddha. "That was my hidden secret, which you could not have survived."

The monster was so moved that he became Prince Five Weapons' disciple from that day on. He learned the Eightfold Path. With the dawn of inner peace, he lost his violent nature. He learned that all his monstrous deeds were the result of past bad actions which could be atoned for. In the end Sticky Hair became enlightened, and thus the villagers were rescued from their monster in the woods.

The same hidden secret could save us if we turn to it. In thousands and thousands of hearts around the world compassion is doing its work. The opposite of compassion has to be renounced, because in anger, vengeance, mechanized death, and violence against Nature is our doom. War won't end from any other cure. It won't be suffering that ends war, or the reckless hope of achieving total victory over evil. The real work for peace is proceeding one person at a time and eventually tipping the balance in the world. History has already sent beacons of compassion in Christ, Buddha, Lao-Tze, and countless saints from every faith, including Islam. We don't need any more beacons. The message doesn't need delivering one more time.

You and I and many others feel no need for war, no satisfaction in it, and no allure. We got ourselves unstuck from Sticky Hair's fur. Every person who gets unstuck is one unit of peace. I don't know how many units it takes to change the world. The ogre who devours humans doesn't want for victims. But the most horrific weapons have all been tried, and now is the time to use the secret hidden inside. You and I are nothing compared to the huge machinery of mechanized death that has overwhelmed us. But we know that our hidden secret is real, and we should celebrate: ours is the one weapon that will surely blow up the monster.

Appendix

The Program for Peacemakers

THE FOLLOWING IS a pamphlet outlining the weekly program for peacemakers that appears in "The Way of Peace," page 7. It's offered here as reference for anyone interested in becoming part of a community of consciousness The same materials can be downloaded from *www.chopra.com,* where it appears in printable form under News from Deepak.

SEVEN PRACTICES FOR PEACEMAKERS

*How to end war
one person at a time*

WAR IS THE plague that human beings bring upon themselves. It is also a plague we might be able to end. On any given day since you and I were born, some part of the world has been at war; in 2003 the total number of open conflicts was thirty. In the twentieth century at least 108 million people died in wars. Of the

twenty largest military budgets on earth, fourteen belong to developing countries. The United States spends more on its military than the next sixteen countries combined.

That war is the major problem in the world is undeniable.

The need for a new idea is just as undeniable.

The new idea is to bring peace one person at a time until
the world reaches a critical mass of peacemakers instead of warmakers.

There is no way to peace. Peace is the way.

MAHATMA GANDHI

Why Ending War Hasn't Worked

PEACE MOVEMENTS HAVE tried three ways for bringing war to
an end:

Activism, the approach of putting political pressure on governments that wage war. Activism involves protests and public
demonstrations, lobbying and political commitment. Almost
every war creates some kind of peace movement opposed to it.

Why has it failed?

Because the protesters are not heard.

Because they are worn down by frustration and resistance.

Because they are far outnumbered by the war interests in
society.

Because their idealism turns to anger and violence.

Activism has left us with the ironic picture of outraged
peacemakers who wind up contributing to the total sum of violence in the world.

THE SECOND APPROACH is *humanitarianism,* the approach of helping the victims of war. Bringing relief to victims is an act of kindness and compassion. As embodied by the International Red Cross, this effort is ongoing and attracts thousands of volunteers worldwide. Every nation on earth approves of humanitarianism.

Why has it failed?

Because humanitarians are wildly outnumbered by soldiers and warmakers.

Because of finances. The International Red Cross annual budget of $1.8 billion dollars is a tiny fraction of military budgets around the world.

Because the same countries that wage war also conduct humanitarian efforts, keeping the two activities very separate.

Because humanitarians show up on the scene after the war has already begun.

THE THIRD APPROACH is *personal transformation,* the approach of ending war one person at a time. The prevailing idea is that war begins in each human heart and can only end there. The religious tradition of praying for peace is the closest most people will ever come to ending war in their own hearts. Most people have actually never heard of this approach.

Why has it failed?

Because nobody has really tried it.

Can you be the change that you wish to see in the world?

MAHATMA GANDHI

Why War Ends with You

THE APPROACH OF personal transformation is the idea of the future for ending war. It depends on the only advantage that people of peace have over warmakers: sheer numbers. If enough people in the world transformed themselves into peacemakers, war could end. The leading idea here is **critical mass.** It took a critical mass of human beings to embrace electricity and fossil fuels, to teach evolution and adopt every major religion. When the time is right and enough people participate, critical mass can change the world.

Can it end war?

There is precedent to believe that it might. The ancient Indian ideal of *Ahimsa,* or nonviolence, gave Gandhi his guiding principle of reverence for life. In every spiritual tradition it is believed that peace must exist in one's heart before it can exist in the outer world.

Personal transformation deserves a chance.

When a person is established in nonviolence,
those in his vicinity cease to feel hostility.

PATANJALI, ANCIENT INDIAN SAGE

SEVEN PRACTICES FOR PEACE

THE PROGRAM FOR peacemakers asks you to follow a specific practice every day, each one centered on the theme of peace.

Sunday: Being for Peace
Monday: Thinking for Peace
Tuesday: Feeling for Peace

Wednesday: Speaking for Peace
Thursday: Acting for Peace
Friday: Creating for Peace
Saturday: Sharing for Peace

Our hope is that you will create peace on every level of your life. Each practice takes only a few minutes. You can be as private or outspoken as you wish. But those around you will know that you are for peace, not just through good intentions but by the way you conduct your life on a daily basis.

Sunday: Being for Peace

TODAY, TAKE FIVE minutes to meditate for peace. Sit quietly with your eyes closed. Put your attention on your heart and inwardly repeat these four words: *Peace, Harmony, Laughter, Love.* Allow these words to radiate from your hearts stillness out into your body.

As you end your meditation, say to yourself, *Today I will relinquish all resentments and grievances.* Bring into your mind anyone against whom you have a grievance and let it go. Send that person your forgiveness.

Monday: Thinking for Peace

THINKING HAS POWER when it is backed by intention. Today, introduce the intention of peace in your thoughts. Take a few moments of silence, then repeat this ancient prayer:

> *Let me be loved, let me be happy, let me be peaceful.*
>
> *Let my friends be happy, loved, and peaceful.*
>
> *Let my perceived enemies be happy, loved, and peaceful.*
>
> *Let all beings be happy, loved, and peaceful.*
>
> *Let the whole world experience these things.*

If at any time during the day you are overshadowed by fear or anger, repeat these intentions. Use this prayer to get back on center.

Tuesday: Feeling for Peace

THIS IS THE day to experience the emotions of peace. The emotions of peace are compassion, understanding, and love.

Compassion is the feeling of shared suffering. When you feel someone else's suffering, there is the birth of understanding.

Understanding is the knowledge that suffering is shared by everyone. When you understand that you aren't alone in your suffering, there is the birth of love.

When there is love there is the opportunity for peace.

As your practice, observe a stranger some time during your day. Silently say to yourself, This person is just like me. Like me, this person has experienced joy and sorrow, despair and hope, fear and love. Like me, this person has people in his or her life who deeply care and love him or her. Like me, this person's life is impermanent and will one day end. This person's peace is as important as my peace. I want peace, harmony, laughter, and love in his or her life and the life of all beings.

Wednesday: Speaking for Peace

TODAY, THE PURPOSE of speaking is to create happiness in the listener. Have this intention: Today every word I utter will be chosen consciously. I will refrain from complaints, condemnation, and criticism.

Your practice is to do at least one of the following:

Tell someone how much you appreciate them.
Express genuine gratitude to those who have helped and loved you.

Offer healing or nurturing words to someone who needs them. Show respect to someone whose respect you value.

If you find that you are reacting negatively to anyone, in a way that isn't peaceful, refrain from speaking and keep silent. Wait to speak until you feel centered and calm, and then speak with respect.

Thursday: Acting for Peace

TODAY IS THE day to help someone in need: a child, a sick person, an older or frail person. Help can take many forms. Tell yourself, *Today I will bring a smile to a stranger's face. If someone acts in a hurtful way to me or someone else, I will respond with a gesture of loving kindness. I will send an anonymous gift to someone, however small. I will offer help without asking for gratitude or recognition.*

Friday: Creating for Peace

TODAY, COME UP with at least one creative idea to resolve a conflict, either in your personal life or your family circle or among friends. If you can, try and create an idea that applies to your community, the nation, or the whole world. You may change an old habit that isn't working, look at someone a new way, offer words you never offered before, or think of an activity that brings people together in good feeling and laughter.

Secondly, invite a family member or friend to come up with one creative idea of this kind on his or her own. Creativity feels best when you are the one thinking up the new idea or approach. Make it known that you accept and enjoy creativity. Be loose and easy. Let the ideas flow and try out anything that has appeal. The purpose here is to bond, because only when you bond with others can there be mutual trust. When you trust, there is no need for hidden hostility and suspicion—the two great enemies of peace.

Saturday: Sharing for Peace

TODAY, SHARE YOUR practice of peacemaking with two people. Give them this booklet and invite them to begin the daily practice. As more of us participate in this sharing, our practice will expand into a critical mass.

Today, joyfully celebrate your own peace consciousness with at least one other peace-conscious person. Connect either through e-mail or phone.

Share your experience of growing peace.

Share your gratitude that someone else is as serious about peace as you are.

Share your ideas for helping the world move closer to critical mass.

Do whatever you can, in small or large ways, to assist anyone who wants to become a peacemaker.

The Best Reason to Become a Peacemaker

NOW YOU KNOW the program. If you transform yourself into a peacemaker, you won't become an activist marching in the streets. You will not be anti anything. No money is required. All you are asked to do is to go within and dedicate yourself to peace.

It just might work.

Even if you don't immediately see a decline in violence around the world, you will know in your heart that you have dedicated your own life to peace.

But the single best reason to become a peacemaker is that every other approach has failed.

We don't know what number the critical mass is—the best we can hope is to bring about change by personal transformation. Isn't it worth a few moments of your day to end thirty wars around the world and perhaps every future war that is certain to break out?

Right now there are 21.3 million soldiers serving in armies around the world. Can't we recruit a peace brigade ten times larger?

A hundred times larger?

The effort begins now, with you.

Notes

I WROTE THIS book by keeping my eyes and ears open. A novice in the details of the war machine, I found the Internet an invaluable help. Most of the facts in these pages were Googled, and therefore by entering the same key words, any reader can discover the information I was led to. The Internet has a reputation for recklessness, but in fact it is often more reliable than a conventional library. Every fact can be checked many times over. For example, if you enter the phrase "Iraqi body count 2004," Google delivers 25,000 entries, and they are more up to date than any printed book.

I also kept a diary of daily events in the world. I derived my information from Web news sources, primarily AOL News and the Associated Press releases that can be found at many online sources such as *www.salon.com.*

I hope that readers who wish to pursue an individual topic will go to the Web and investigate for themselves, because only by keeping your eyes and ears open can you expand your consciousness. In the chapter on religion and its failure to end war I mention my appearance on the *Larry King Live* show with four religious leaders. Each of them kept referring to our duty to fight evil, and at the last moment I let out a protest, which was largely drowned out by their voices: "We have to stop calling other people evil." By exploring the wealth of information on war that is available on the Web, you will also dive into new worlds and new perspectives. Being trapped in our cultural blindness is the same as being stuck in Sticky Hair's fur.

A good place to begin is the site where I began my own search: "What Every Person Should Know About War." But I hope your trail leads to the Web site of Aljazeera, the controversial Arab satellite TV network, so that you can find out for yourself what the Arab world is thinking and how it sees us. I probably don't need to mention the free online sites of *Time, Newsweek,* and *The New York Times,* plus less mainstream sources like Salon.com and Slate.com. But how many of us go to the Internet to read *The Times* of London, or *The Observer*? One discovers very quickly that our view of Europe has become distorted and oversimplified.

If you are psychologically minded, check out "A Fine Line Between Normal and Monster?" which is a fascinating online article, one of many to be found on the Millgram pain experiment and the Stanford prison experiment. The historically minded can follow numerous threads to Adolf Eichmann, Osip Mandelstam, and medieval weaponry at the Battle of Crecy, all of which I barely touched upon in these pages. If you are scientifically minded, I fervently urge you to read one book, *The Self-Aware Universe* by Amit Goswami. More than any other contemporary physicist, his explanation of the tangled hierarchy has altered my view of how reality is constructed. It has been a privilege to discuss this concept with him over the past five years.

Finally, reading about Hannah Arendt and her famous thoughts on the banality of evil will help convince anyone of the everyday ways in which the tangled hierarchy enmeshes us all.

Arendt was not an optimistic thinker, given the long shadow of the Holocaust. But she did say something hopeful: that deep reflection will bring us face to face with the decisions we make and turn our choices away from evil. The way of peace is about more than deep reflection. Yet the path begins there, and to that end I have written this book.

What Can I Do?

OUR TASK TOGETHER is to form a peace movement that isn't an antiwar movement. The difference is crucial, because every movement founded to be "anti" has led in the end to resistance, opposition, and violence. I can only speak as one person, but my ideal of a peace movement is based on one of the three S-words: Satsang. Satsang means sharing your consciousness with other people. It can begin with something as simple as holding a discussion group once a week, an open forum in which everyone gets a chance to speak about their own desire for peace.

The next step might be a "peace cell," a group of ten people who want to further peace through the seven-step program outlined in this book. To that end, I've included a pamphlet on page 241 entitled "The Program for Peacemakers" that can be downloaded from the Internet and circulated to anyone who might want to be part of a peace cell.

Finally, as consciousness grows, you might want to join a global community of peace cells. A special website, www.peaceisthewayglobalcommunity.org, has been set up to list each peace cell and provide links for them to have Satsang around the world.

I would love to see my ideal become a reality, but the whole point of a peace movement is to participate according to your ideal. Peace is a vision, and visions must grow on their own, following one's inner desires. Right now the vision is a spark, but somewhere, sometime, the spark will catch flame. I can't say when that moment will be—it could be with you. I hope so, because I know with certainty that there is no stronger community than the invisible one created by people inspired by their own highest purpose.

Index

A

Abu Ghraib prison, 183, 221
adrenaline, 205
Afghanistan, 175, 208
Africa, 51, 58
Age of Exploration, 22
aggression, male, 199–200
aging process, 206
AIDS, 51, 71
Albanians, 123–24
American identity
  criticism of, 52
  falsehoods about, 53–55
  features of, 55–56
  illusions and realities of, 57–58
  implications about, 52
American Revolution, 57–58
anger, chemistry of, 127–30
anger, releasing
  ceasing to fixate on old hurt,
    136–37
  finding a new identity, 141
  finding deeper sense of self,
    138–40
  finding new ways to be happy,
    131–32
  gaining a new vision, 137–38
  learning to forgive, 132–35

  not depending on others, 136–37
  overview of, 130–31
animal nature, in humans, 100–103,
    199–200
anti-Semitism, 90–91, 147–49
apathy, ending, 220–21
Arafat, Yasser, 174, 190, 194
Armstrong, Eugene, 169–70
atom bombs, 3, 78, 84

B

Baba, Meher, 216, 236
Basayev, Shamil, 64
belief systems, 197–98
belligerent actions, ceasing, 195
Berlin Wall, 9, 21
Bernardo, Francesco, 74–76
Beslan attack, 63–64, 85, 87,
    154–55
bin Laden, Osama, 64, 85, 173
Blake, William, 91
Bloom, Paul, 113
bombs, 3, 73, 78, 84
Bosnia, 216
Boykin, William, 176–77
brain chemistry, 103–7, 199–200,
    206

A NOTE ABOUT THE TYPE

This book was set in Mrs. Eaves, a modern revival of Baskerville that retains the openness and lightness of the original. In 1996, when Zuzano Licko, cofounder of Emigre Foundry, designed the typeface, her aim was to explore possible alternatives for Baskerville, which critics claimed was illegible due to the high contrast in its stems and hairlines. Licko reduced the contrast by widening the proportions of the lowercase letters. Mrs. Eaves was one of the first digital typefaces to be designed on Apple's Macintosh computers. The typeface is named after Sarah Eaves, who was first housekeeper and, later, wife and partner to John Baskerville in his print and type shop.

COMPOSED BY
Stratford Publishing Services, Inc.
Brattleboro, Vermont

PRINTED AND BOUND BY
Berryville Graphics
Berryville, Virginia